What Readers Are Saying About
Pomodoro Technique Illustrated

Staffan gives us the theory and practice of Francesco Cirillo's Pomodoro Technique in an enjoyable package with wonderful illustrations. This is a delightful and useful book!

➤ **Ron Jeffries**
   www.XProgramming.com

The Pomodoro Technique is amazing in its simplicity and its power to make you more productive, and this book is the perfect introduction to the technique.

➤ **Dave Klein**
   Author, *Grails: A Quick-Start Guide*

Thank you for such a beautiful and thoughtful book! It's on my Christmas list for my friends.

➤ **Portia Tung**
   Agile Consultant-Coach and Chief Strategy Officer, emergn

The Pomodoro Technique is the one action-planning technique that fits exactly as conceived into Agile approaches to projects. If you want to learn the technique and become excellent at it, you need this book. Staffan brings humor, examples, and a step-by-step approach to making the Pomodoro Technique work for you. Your overall estimates will become better, and you'll get more work done.

➤ **Johanna Rothman**
   Author, Consultant

This is an easy read with a life-changing message to all of us who have "too much to do and not enough time." Since Staffan introduced me to the Pomodoro Technique, I have become a better person, both professionally and in my private life. This is a book I wish I had read years ago!

➤ **Thomas Nilsson**
  CTO, Agile Mentor, Responsive Development Technologies AB

Pomodoro Technique Illustrated

The Easy Way to Do More in Less Time

Staffan Nöteberg

The Pragmatic Bookshelf

Dallas, Texas • Raleigh, North Carolina

Many of the designations used by manufacturers and sellers to distinguish their products are claimed as trademarks. Where those designations appear in this book, and The Pragmatic Programmers, LLC was aware of a trademark claim, the designations have been printed in initial capital letters or in all capitals. The Pragmatic Starter Kit, The Pragmatic Programmer, Pragmatic Programming, Pragmatic Bookshelf, PragProg and the linking *g* device are trademarks of The Pragmatic Programmers, LLC.

Every precaution was taken in the preparation of this book. However, the publisher assumes no responsibility for errors or omissions, or for damages that may result from the use of information (including program listings) contained herein.

Our Pragmatic courses, workshops, and other products can help you and your team create better software and have more fun. For more information, as well as the latest Pragmatic titles, please visit us at *http://pragprog.com*.

Printed in the United States of America.
ISBN-13: 978-1-934356-50-0
Printed on acid-free paper.
Book version: P3.0—November 2013

Contents

Foreword by Francesco Cirillo

Who doesn't want to have a stress-free life? To have brilliant ideas? To improve? To enjoy free time? But how can we achieve these goals? Often frequent interruptions, overlapping activities, and impending deadlines prevent us from the best intentions. In fact, stressful factors like these are harmful to us; they trigger more stress, compulsive behavior, and discontinuity, and they reduce our consciousness, concentration, and clear-minded thinking. The mind ends up wandering forward and backward in time, looking for someone or something to blame for our imagined inability.

The Pomodoro Technique that I've developed aims to make us stop, observe, regain awareness, and, in doing so, improve ourselves. Time, rather than being a stress-inducing factor, becomes our ally in keeping the mind 100 percent focused on the present with no stress and no strain. With my Pomodoro Technique, you'll learn to reach your goals by being strong, instead of exerting strength, and doing so with a smile.

Staffan is a serious practitioner of the Pomodoro Technique. I've been working for many years with people and groups that want to improve their working processes and optimize their time through the Pomodoro Technique, and I can say that Staffan's work is proof of his ability and imagination. With this book, I am impressed by how Staffan has succeeded in visually representing the concepts of my technique; readers will appreciate and benefit from his expertise. The content is informative, easy to use, stimulating, and effective. A real treasure! Enjoy!

Ring!

Francesco Cirillo, 2009

CEO at XPLabs SRL in Rome

Creator of the Pomodoro Technique

http://www.pomodorotechnique.com

Foreword by Henrik Kniberg

[Winding up the clock. Tick-tick-tick...]

A couple of days each week I schedule "slack" days where I catch up on emails, prepare for upcoming engagements, and do other desk work. The first thing I do is decide whether I need to be effective that day. Today I wanted to be effective, so I selected eight Pomodori worth of items from my Activity Inventory sheet and added them to today's To Do Today sheet.

I used to think I could do 12 Pomodori in a day (that's "only" six hours, after all), but reality has shown me that eight is more realistic, since the Pomodoro Technique counts only focused time. Reality is a great but sometimes harsh teacher. I used to think course preparation took two Pomodori. It turned out it took four every time—at least twice as long as I originally thought. That triggered me to find ways to do it more effectively, so now I'm down to three. The Pomodoro Technique has helped me plan better, get more stuff done with less stress, and have more time for family and hobbies.

[Opening my blog to see what I wrote earlier about the Pomodoro Technique. Oh, look—a comment has come in! Wait! Don't read the comment now. I'm in a Pomodoro, right? I'm supposed to focus on writing the foreword. I'll get back to that comment later. Mark the internal interruption.]

If my wife, Sia, sees that my egg timer is ticking, she knows not to interrupt me unnecessarily. She knows that the clock will ring within 12 to 13 minutes (on average), at which time I'll take a short break and go give her a hug, rewarding myself for finishing a Pomodoro and her for letting me.

Does that sound silly? Well, yes, it feels a bit silly having a dumb egg timer dictating what you do. That's why I have to decide every day whether I want to be effective that day. The Pomodoro Technique really helps, though, so a slight feeling of silliness is usually worth it. In fact, sometimes a bit of silliness is a good way to remember that life isn't primarily about getting through your to-do lists.

If I choose not to be effective that day, I leave the egg timer in the drawer. I'll have a relaxing day of procrastination, with no self-imposed discipline. Then at least I'm not kidding myself and...

[BRRRRIIIIING. Pomodoro is over...let me just complete that sentence.]

...building up false expectations about getting things done.

[X. No hug—Sia is gone today. Go play bass for a few minutes. Back again. So, should I continue writing or check that blog comment? No, I'm in a flow. Keep writing; the blog can wait. Winding up the clock. Tick-tick-tick...]

The Pomodoro Technique is similar to Agile methods such as Scrum and XP but at a "micro" level. It feels sort of like being a single-person team doing 25-minute iterations. The main difference is that, in Agile methods, velocity usually means how much stuff gets done per iteration. In the Pomodoro Technique, velocity means how many Pomodori get done per day. You get lots of stuff done, not by focusing on getting stuff done but by focusing on focusing!

Thanks, Staffan, for introducing the Pomodoro Technique to me! I'm glad to see that it is getting popular, because it's another useful tool for the process tool kit.

Oh, and about this book: if you are perfectly disciplined and efficient already, this book might not help you. At the other extreme, if you are completely undisciplined, you might not even get through the book, much less succeed in following the rules of the Pomodoro Technique. But most likely you are like the rest of us and somewhere in the middle. In that case, I congratulate you! Not only will Staffan's book help you improve, but the personal anecdotes and great illustrations will make it a pleasant journey! Enjoy. :o)

[Go back to polishing the text a bit...]

[BRRRIIIIIING. X. OK, good enough to send as a first draft to Staffan.]

Henrik Kniberg, 2009

Agile & Lean process coach at Crisp in Stockholm

Agile Alliance board member

Author of *Scrum and XP from the Trenches*

One Activity at a Time

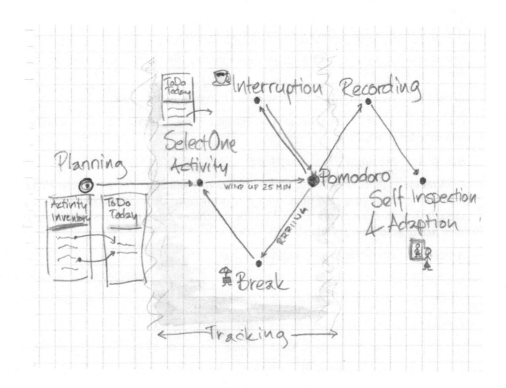

1.1 A Cucumber and an Artichoke Meet at a Bar

Cucumber: How was work today?

Artichoke: Terrible. I didn't get anything done.

Cucumber: Why? Don't you have anything to do?

Artichoke: I do! I need to complete and deliver a new printing feature. I planned to get it done today.

Cucumber: But you didn't do that?

Artichoke: No, I was constantly interrupted with requests to do other things.

Cucumber: And were these requests more important than completing your printing feature?

Artichoke: Actually, I don't know. I didn't compare.

Cucumber: And you completed nothing—neither the printing feature nor the important requests?

Artichoke: How could I complete so many things in just one day?

Cucumber: I didn't ask whether you completed many things; I asked whether you completed anything.

Artichoke: No, nothing was completed.

Cucumber: I think you should try the Pomodoro Technique. You focus on a single activity for 25 minutes and then, after a short break, compare any new requests with the one you were working on. You see which one has the highest priority and then follow your new priorities.

Artichoke: I'm ready to give anything a try!

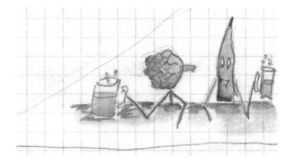

1.2 Getting Started

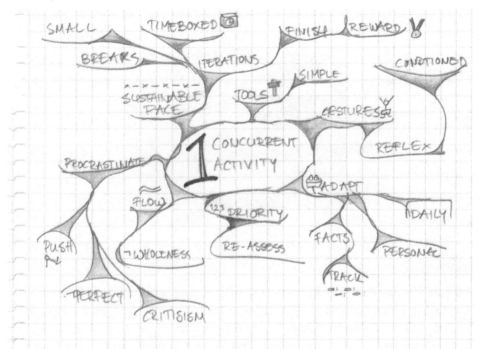

Getting thoughts out of your head is mandatory if you want to be able to stay focused.

Throughout this book, I describe my own experiences with the Pomodoro Technique. You will learn all about how to implement the technique and along the way hear how it improved my own productivity. In addition, I include research on the human mind that explains why this technique works, some of the consequences of adopting the technique, and ways in which you may want to adapt or extend the technique.

This first chapter begins with a few stories and a chance for you to experience the technique. I want you to try a hands-on exercise early to give you context for understanding the rest of the book. I end this chapter with an inventory of *symptoms* in my life that helped me understand I needed to better focus my time and efforts. You may recognize yourself in this catalog. My story begins with a bus ride.

1.3   Bus Time

I live in a suburb of Stockholm. Since I'm a consultant, I mostly work at a client's big office somewhere downtown. There's a bus stop just 100 meters from my house. Every morning starts exactly the same: I go to the bus stop and wait for the bus to come. When it arrives, I step on and sit down in my usual seat. The trip downtown takes about 25 minutes, and I always use it for reading a nonfiction book related to my work.

During these 25 minutes, it's impossible to get a cup of coffee, to turn on the TV, to check my favorite Internet community, or to do anything else that suddenly turns up to be so dramatically important when I try to read that same book at home. Furthermore, I don't know the people traveling on my bus. I might occasionally say "Hello" to a familiar face, but that's all, so there are no other distractions.

My reading time on the bus is a *timeboxed*, single-activity, single-goal experience with amazing results. I never learn as much as during my morning bus trip. I focus 100 percent on the book and trust that the bus driver will tell me when it's time to stop reading.

I can't ride a bus back and forth all day long just to achieve this level of productivity, and neither can you. Fortunately, we don't have to. The Pomodoro Technique will help you split up your day into little bus rides like this. You just decide where you are traveling on your mini bus ride, set the timer, and focus on your work.

1.4   The Tomato-Shaped Timer

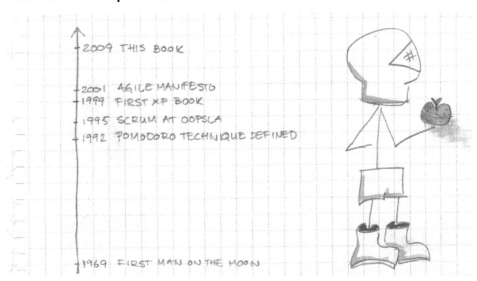

Francesco Cirillo defined the Pomodoro Technique in 1992, but it all started in the late 1980s, during his first years at college. The breakthrough came out of frustration over his low productivity and unstructured studying—thanks to a red, round object that made a ringing noise:

"I made a bet with myself, and it was as helpful as it was humiliating. I asked myself, 'Can I study—really study—for 10 minutes?' I needed objective validation—a time tutor—and I found one in a kitchen timer shaped like a pomodoro (the Italian word for "tomato"). In other words, I found my Pomodoro."[1]

With the Pomodoro Technique, you can make time your friend, not your enemy. Instead of feeling anxiety about deadlines for this hour, this day, this week, or this month, you set a timer for 25 minutes and completely focus on the task at hand. When the timer rings at the end of the 25 minutes and you're still working, it does not mean that you have failed to finish. On the contrary. It is a round of applause for your completed timebox.

In a nutshell, that's what the Pomodoro Technique is—decide on the tasks you will do that day, set a timer for 25 minutes, and then start the first one. You'll also have daily retrospectives, create daily commitments, handle interruptions, and estimate the effort put forth. This book will walk you through how I do the technique, including how to record your activities and pick the tasks that are the most important.

---

1.   *The Pomodoro Technique [Cir06]*

1.5 Try It Now: Timeboxed Activity

It sounds easy, but let's try a timeboxed activity to get you into the swing of things. Get a piece of paper and a pen. Make a list of several activities that you might have been doing right now if you weren't busy reading this book. It could be a form to fill out for your child's school, something you wanted to look up on the Web, an email that you must write, or some other administrative task.

Now, which one of the tasks that you wrote down is most important? Which one would you prefer to have completed? Bookmark this page, and follow these steps to work on that task:

1. Wind up your kitchen timer for 10 minutes.
2. Concentrate only on that particular task.
3. Stop immediately when the timer rings, even if the task is not completed.
4. Take a three-minute break, and then continue reading this book.

How did it go? Were you able to avoid thinking about other things during those 10 minutes? How often did you look at the timer?

When using the Pomodoro Technique, you typically wind up the timer for 25-minute timeboxes. If you want, you can try to read the rest of the book in exactly that way: read the book in 25-minute iterations—controlled by your kitchen timer, of course—and then spend three minutes of relaxation in between the reading periods.

1.6   Max, My Father's Grandfather

Max moved to Berlin in the early 20th century to start a company that manufactured clothes. The company thrived, and his guiding principle contributed to his success. He lived by the following maxim: "You can't dance at two weddings with one rear end." In other words, you should focus on one activity at a time.

Think of Max's maxim and the Pomodoro Technique as a total denial of simultaneous capacity—an axiomatic boundary. How can you then be sure that what you're doing is the most important activity? Well, for me, first I analyze what really matters, in other words, what result I want to achieve. Then I start to focus on the activity that will lead me to this result. But just before I start to focus, I wind up a timer. It will wake me up later. And I can then reanalyze: is the activity that I focused on still the one that matters most?

Max was definitively a forerunner when it comes to modern attention management techniques!

1.7   Why the Pomodoro Technique?

Let me tell you a little bit about why I started using the Pomodoro Technique so that you can assess whether it might work for you. Before implementing the technique, time just seemed to disappear, poof! Much of what I intended to get done during the day remained undone. When I looked more carefully, I was able to identify many symptoms that needed treating. In fact, I bet you are familiar with one or two of them. The following are the problems that can cause people to not get work done. The rest of the book describes how the good practices of the Pomodoro Technique can help you solve them.

Excitement decreases when complexity is high. When tasks are complex, you can't complete them in a single 25-minute period, so you tend to procrastinate. Procrastination provides easy relief when problems are hard—but the problems don't go away. No matter how complex the task, the important thing is to keep starting. Wind up the clock, and within a half hour you will have accomplished something and get rewarded with a break.

Procrastination increases when tasks are boring. If you don't complete activities, they won't give you any value. Of course, doing the last bit of cleaning up always feels boring. But don't think about how much you have left to do of this activity. Imagine instead how quickly you'll finish off one Pomodoro. After that, you'll be rewarded.

The hard work is done, but the activities that matter are still not completed. With the Pomodoro Technique, you do your planning in the morning and commit to doing a small number of activities that day. Then you reassess your priorities before every *Pomodoro*, one single activity that is the outstandingly most important activity to complete. You will always be doing the thing that matters most and nothing else.

The pressure builds before a deadline. Long hours and working weekends are never productive in the long run. If you are forced to put in more hours than what you're comfortable with, you won't be able to produce quality work for long. You can create a sustainable pace with the Pomodoro Technique rhythm by using short iterations of 25 minutes, by not skipping breaks, and by focusing on one activity at a time.

The mental transition between work and breaks is too slow. Sometimes you can lose time during the day just getting started or just coming back from lunch. The time it takes to get back on task can add up before you know it. The Pomodoro Technique is gesture-oriented. Do wind up the clock. Do have a personal ring signal. Do write the To Do Today sheet as an easy-to-grasp reference. Conditioned reflexes are great tools.

Mistakes get repeated over and over. To avoid the same errors day after day, the last three stages of the Pomodoro Technique are done at the end of every day. Record, Process, and Visualize are together the daily retrospective and the key points for adapting your personal process, which means you learn and improve every day. It also means you can start from the textbook version of the Pomodoro Technique and then adapt it to suit your individual work context as you get more familiar with your working habits.

The effort that one task takes is underestimated. Activities become much clearer when they are broken down into smaller items. If you estimate that an activity will need more than seven Pomodori, you can break it down. Using Pomodori estimating, you can get immediate feedback on the pace at which you are working when you compare your Pomodori estimate with the actual number of completed Pomodori per activity. This is called *quantity estimating.*

The scope of a task is underestimated. Do secondary tasks spin off from your activities while you work on them? No problem, with the Pomodoro Technique, you just add them to the Unplanned & Urgent list and then intensify your efforts to complete the main activity. This is called *quality estimating.*

Your mind is invaded by competing thoughts. Sometimes it's hard to focus on one activity because you get so many other great ideas all the time. Just write them down under Unplanned & Urgent, and then intensify your efforts in completing the activity that you're working on. Getting competing thoughts out of your head is mandatory if you want to be able to stay focused.

A complex and demanding methodology of working consumes your time. The Pomodoro Technique is so easy to use that even my preschool daughters understand it. You don't need fancy tools. You don't spend half the day completing process artifacts. You don't need a process coach on-site to explain the comprehensive terminology. And what's more, it's adaptable. You should change it every day to avoid doing unnecessary routines.

You forget about the wholeness while in the flow. The brain needs time to stabilize memories, see patterns, and make conclusions. While practicing the Pomodoro Technique, you take a break every half hour. This gives your brain a chance to absorb what you saw during the last Pomodoro. When you come back, you can see the overall picture and will probably have at least three new ideas.

Estimates are seen as promises. It's impossible to guess exactly how much time an exploratory or development activity will take. You can only make a best guess. The habit of seeing your guess as a promise—either by yourself or by co-workers—creates unnecessary anxiety. To avoid this trap, the Pomodoro Technique counts only the Pomodoro. After 25 minutes of effort, you can focus on your activities even when you're close to a deadline.

Nonetheless, you should provide regular updates on your progress for all stakeholders to see.

The process is not based on facts. You collect process metrics during the day; this is called the Tracking stage. These can be used in the daily retrospective to improve your process tomorrow. It's up to you what you decide to track. It depends on your current work situation, but start off by counting your interruptions and completed Pomodori.

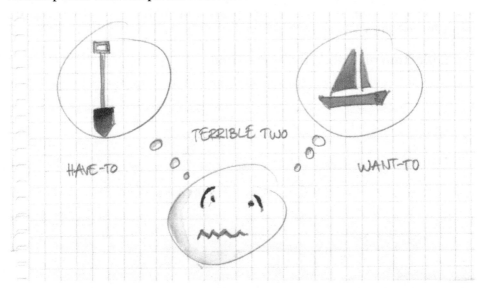

Someone pushes work on you. When people push work on you that you really don't want to do, it's unlikely you'll enjoy doing it. The fight between "have-to" and "want-to" is known as the *terrible two.*[2] Here's a third option. In the Pomodoro Technique, you select a number of activities in the morning that you believe you can complete during the day. By actively pulling activities into your To Do Today sheet instead of getting them pushed on you, you increase your personal commitment.

Perfectionism prevents action. Waiting until you have devised the perfect solution to something is merely a form of procrastination. Procrastination is not an option in the Pomodoro Technique. You just go ahead and get started on a Pomodoro, and you don't have to worry about being "totally perfect." Winding up the clock and putting in 25 minutes of effort will reward you with being able to write an X and then take a break.

2.   *The Now Habit [Fio07]*

Fear of failure or criticism is a mental impediment. The Pomodoro Technique is your commitment, your process metrics, and your process. You don't have to share your version of it with anybody. Find out what works for you. The number of completed Pomodori a day is your tool for working more effectively, completing more, and having more fun while working. It can't be used by your boss to review your performance.

Did you recognize any habits from your office? Most people do. And if all these words like *Pomodori*, *stages*, and *sheets* are gibberish to you, then prepare yourself by reading this book.

1.8   Self-Reflection on One Activity at a Time

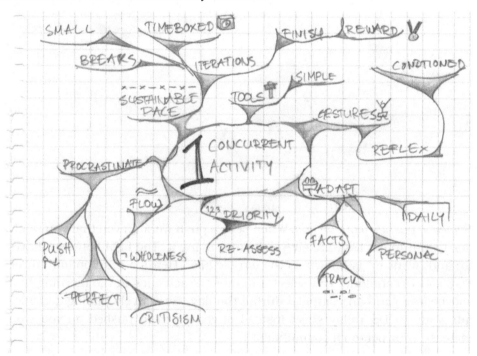

- What makes you stop an activity before you are done?
- Where is the best place to read to help you really focus?
- What do you do to avoid starting on a boring task?
- What type of activities usually take more time than you initially estimated?
- Are you bound to do administrative activities that steal time from more important activities?

CHAPTER 2

Context

2.1   A Cucumber and an Artichoke Meet at the Zoo

Cucumber: *Did you try the Pomodoro Technique?*

Artichoke: *I did. It was great. I got so much done.*

Cucumber: *That's great. I knew you'd like it.*

Artichoke: *I didn't think it would work for me, but it did.*

Cucumber: *Of course it did; it's the way you are wired.*

Artichoke: *What do you mean?*

Cucumber: *You just need to understand a bit more about how your brain works. There are forces in your environment that fight against your nature.*

Artichoke: So, the Pomodoro Technique helps me get control over all of the stimuli I'm getting from my environment?

Cucumber: Exactly. And not only that, but you can benefit from what you've inherited from reptiles.

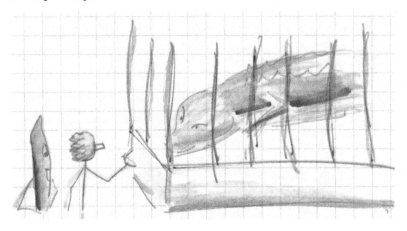

2.2 The Foundation

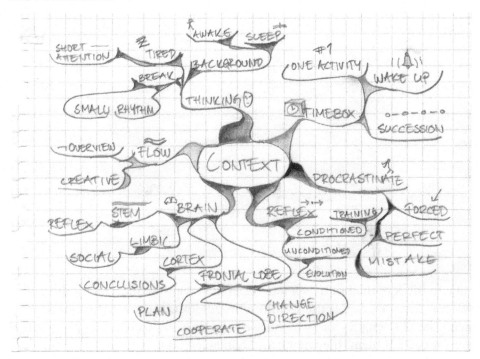

The prospects for getting into the flow are much better when you are rested, seated, and focused than when you are just hanging around and waiting for inspiration.

In this chapter we'll look at what scientists know about you, your brain, and how it works. Read the sections of this chapter as short independent stories, and don't pay too much attention to how you will use this information. Later you'll come to see that the simplicity of the Pomodoro Technique allows you to work with your nature instead of fighting against it.

2.3   The Brain Stack

I like to think of the brain as a four-layered stack: the brain stem, the limbic system, the cortex, and the frontal lobe. All four of these layers have their own special strengths and weaknesses. As long as you can tailor a suitable role for each of them, they make an invincible team.

We inherited our brain stems from our reptile ancestors living hundreds of millions of years ago. The brain stem gives us reliable reflexes without having to instantly use our conscious awareness.

The limbic system is shared with our fellow mammals. It helps us with our long-term memory and also carries reward signals further up. The main themes here are feelings and social connections.

The cortex is more developed in the more intelligent animals like us humans. It makes us aware and conscious. We can see the "big picture" and consequently make conclusions.

The human frontal lobe makes us different. We can imagine and create new things. We can argue and understand other people's arguments. We can plan, cooperate, and change direction.[1]

---

1.   Blink [Gla06]

2.4   Brain Performance

The human brain is refueled every hour with 2 grams of glucose (comparable to a sugar cube), 150 liters of blood transports, and 3 liters of oxygen. Even though our brains are only 2 percent of our body weight, it consumes 20 percent of the oxygen.[2]

Our brains have something like 100 billion nerve cells. They are called *neurons*, and they talk to each other through 100 trillion synaptic connections. The possible number of thought tracks is the digit 1 followed by 800 zeroes![3]

Matching overall human behavior will take about 100 million MIPS of computer power. Deep Blue, the chess machine that played against world chess champion Garry Kasparov in 1997, used specialized chips to process chess moves at a speed equivalent to a 3 million MIPS computer. Extrapolating the increase in processing power of top-of-the-line computers, it has been forecast that computers suitable for humanlike robots will appear in the 2020s.[4]

---

2.   *Hjärnkoll [Lin08]*
3.   *Brain Child [Buz03]*
4.   *When will computer hardware match the human brain? [Mor98]*

2.5 Rhythm

Our bodies feature many rhythms. They help and control us, from the day we are born until the day when we die. The electrical activity produced by our brains, the electrical activity of our heart, and our breathing cycles are just a few examples of our rhythms. The need for food and rest varies predictably. Even hormone levels follow a cyclic schedule.

Social rhythms are also important. To many people, it is a disaster to miss the annual Christmas celebration or a family member's birthday—this despite the fact that there will probably be many more celebrations and birthdays.

Many of our basic rhythms are controlled by the brain stem. We inherited them from the primates that lived a long, long time ago. A regular, rhythmic life is optimal for our brains. Displaced rhythms upset our brains—traveling through time zones gives us jet lag. People living without rhythms tend to be disorientated and anxious.[5]

That doesn't mean everyone has the same rhythm. A long-distance runner has a different rhythm from a sprinter. It's not only a difference in endurance and explosiveness; it's the amount of time until the next break—the next point of rest. This is the *break rhythm*.[6]

5.　*Blink [Gla06]*
6.　*Ten Thoughts About Time [Jö05]*

2.6   Superstition or Focus Enablers?

Adrian Mutu is a great football player. He has played for Juventus, Inter, and Chelsea and has also scored many goals for the Romanian national team. His own explanation for this success is as simple as it is revealing: "Curses cannot touch me because I wear my underwear inside out."

Turk Wendell was a Major League Baseball pitcher for more than 10 years. He played for the Cubs, the Mets, the Phillies, and the Rockies. He had a total of no less than 515 strikeouts. Why did he hide in the dugout during games? It was because he was brushing his teeth between every inning.

John Terry is the long-term skipper of Chelsea as well as the England national football team. He achieved individual awards like a position on the FIFA World Team, PFA Player of the Year, and UEFA Best Club Football Defender. Why? Ask him, and he will tell you how he always listens to the same Usher CD before every game, how he parks in the same lot before every game, and how he ties tape around his socks exactly three times before every game.

Try to switch desks with your neighbor at the office. It will probably interfere with your concentration for the rest of the day. By always preparing with the same gestures and routines, the brain will self-configure into the best mode to solve a particular kind of task.

2.7 Conditioned and Unconditioned Reflexes

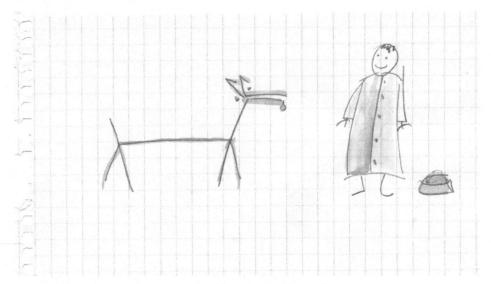

The 1904 Nobel Prize winner Ivan Pavlov made a remarkable discovery by coincidence. He noticed that the dogs in his laboratory tended to salivate when they saw the staff members who usually fed them.

So, Pavlov started a long series of experiments in which he gave dogs various signals just before the presentation of food. It included electric shocks, whistles, metronomes, tuning forks, and also visual stimuli. And, as he expected, after a while the dogs started to salivate every time they received these signals.

A *reflex* is a special signal that creates a specific action. The salivation after hearing a metronome was conditioned by the individual's experience. The dogs learned this reflex from training.

The evolution of species has given us unconditioned reflexes, such as when we blink our eyes. Like conditioned reflexes, the unconditioned are associative. But they are congenital as opposed to the conditioned.

Here's an example in my personal routine: since I brush my teeth every night before I go to bed, I am now sleepy already when I put toothpaste on the toothbrush. Similarly, when using the Pomodoro Technique, I have trained my brain to start to focus as soon as I wind up the kitchen timer and to drop the focus when it rings. Even the ticking sound now reinforces my concentration. These are conditioned reflexes.

2.8   Left Brain and Right Brain

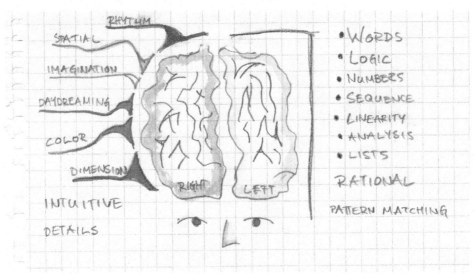

The cerebral cortex covers the two cerebral hemispheres, popularly known as the *left brain* and the *right brain*. If we unfolded and then flattened out our 3mm-thick cortexes, they would be the same size as a tabloid-sized sheet of paper.

A deep groove separates the left brain from the right brain. Nobel Prize winner Roger Sperry discovered in the 1960s that the two hemispheres divide the major intellectual functions between them. Each hemisphere is dominant in certain activities, but they are both basically skilled in all areas.[7]

In our left brain, we tend to match what we see now with what we have experienced before. If a pattern seems rational, then we add it to our repertoire. When we speak, our left brain helps us produce a linear sequence of words that follows syntactic and semantic rules. And analyzing the past is also a typical left-brain task.

Our right brains, on the other hand, are more often intuitive. The right brain understands metaphors, creates dreams, creates new combinations of ideas, and can sometimes give us a eureka moment—from logical disorder.

---

7.   *The Mind Map Book [BB96]*

2.9 Savant

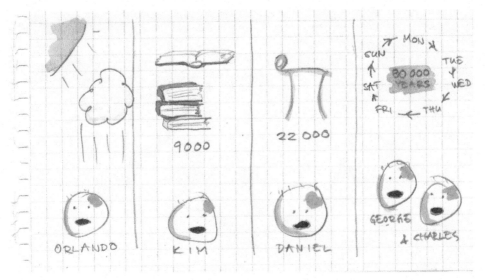

John Langdon Down coined the phrase *idiot savant*, which is French for "knowing idiot," in the 19th century. He studied people with low IQs but exceptional abilities in remembering details.[8] Here are a few examples:

- *Orlando* was an ordinary guy until the age of 10 when he was hit by a baseball on the left side of his head. Since then, he can remember the weather conditions for each and every day that has passed.

- *Kim* couldn't walk until the age of four. But he can now recall the complete text of more than 9,000 books.

- *Daniel* could recite π from memory to more than 22,000 digits.[9]

- *George and Charles*—a pair of identical twins—needed only one second to work out the weekday of an arbitrary day within the past 80,000 years.

Most of the savants either have left-brain damage or lack nerves that connect the two hemispheres. One theory is that the right hemisphere is trying to compensate for this. So, if I see the world through an abstraction filter woven from my own experiences, does that hide an unexpected and astonishing skill in memorizing and calculating things?

---

8. *What autism tells us about development of savant skills. [Rev09]*
9. *Born on a Blue Day [Tam06]*

2.10 Hyperactivity

If you find it very hard to focus all your attention into one single activity for a prolonged period of time, then you have one of the typical symptoms of a hyperactive person. Other indicators could be that you easily become angry or happy or that you have impulsive behavior. It doesn't really matter whether it's nature or nurture that made you this way; the key point is, what can you do about it?

One of the responsibilities of *dopamine*, a neurotransmitter, is to keep people alert. One theory, which could explain why some people are so often hyperactive, is that reduced dopamine production is compensated in the brain by increased production of adrenaline.

For example, when I get really tired, I show similar symptoms as a hyperactive person. My energy resource has run dry, and I'm responding with a short span of attention. Therefore, I need to rest to get new energy. To be optimally attentive, I need small breaks every half hour and not more than a 40-hour/week work schedule. My experience has taught me that working at a sustainable pace is a prerequisite if I want to produce great results.

2.11 Working Memory

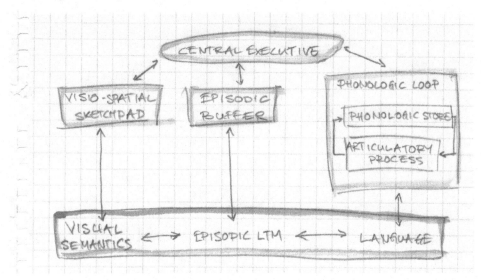

Can you remember a sequence of more than seven digits? Alan Baddeley created a theoretical construct in 1974 that describes the structures and processes in the brain that are used for temporarily storing and manipulating information.

The Central Executive controls our cognitive processes and channels information further. It's our CEO. The Phonological Loop stores what we see by rehearsing it. Its limited nature makes short words easier to remember. The Visio-spatial Sketchpad keeps information about what we see. It helps us judge distance or imagine images. The Episodic Buffer is our generalist. It links across domains, creating integrated visual, spatial, verbal, and chronological units. It's a pretty good friend with our long-term memory as well.

The working memory is limited. For example, I can't focus on two problems simultaneously. If I'm working on a task and my attention is suddenly caught by something else, then when I return to what I was doing, I waste time getting back up to speed with it. That's why changing context too often reduces results. The Pomodoro Technique helps you avoid having your limited working memory become a bottleneck.[10]

---

10. *The Overflowing Brain [Kli08]*

2.12 Association Machine

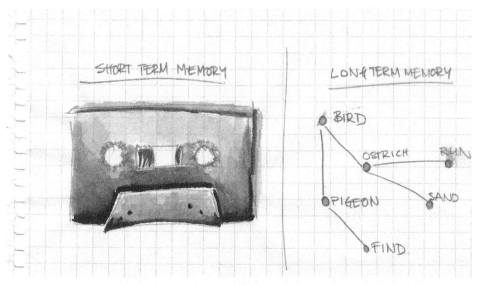

Alan Baddeley showed in 1966 in his study of memory encoding that information is normally stored as sound in the short-term memory.[11] This is opposed to long-term memory where the information is normally stored semantically. Long-term memory is like a gigantic association machine.

For instance, immediately recalling a group of words like *cat, hat, fat, rat* is much harder than immediately recalling *little, small, tiny, modest*. The latter words are acoustically different and are easier to distinguish for our working memory's Phonological Loop.

Delaying the recall a day turns this truth upside down. With delayed recall, it's easier to remember words with dissimilar meaning. We encode our memories as associations. Visual techniques such as mind maps are an excellent tool for pinpointing associations, which are suitable for long-term memory.

---

11. *Short-term memory for word sequences as a function of acoustic, semantic and formal similarity.* [Bad66]

2.13 Succession and Duration

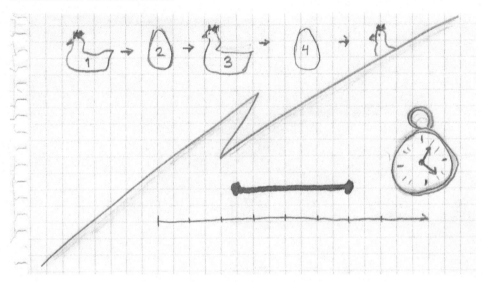

Think about two different aspects of time:

- *Time as duration*: "I've been shopping for two hours, and I'm still not done" or "Oh, I need to catch a bus in 10 minutes" or "How long will it take you to complete this activity?" This is time as a distance between two points —the start and end points.

- *Time as succession*: Hen 1 laid egg 2. Egg 2 was hatched, and hen 3 was born. Hen 3 laid egg 4, and so on. These are nonoverlapping events. We don't know when they happened, but we know the sequence.

Thinking, planning, and calculating future time as a duration is very unpredictable—at least when it comes to doing things that we haven't done before in the same way. For me and for most people, this property of unpredictability produces anxiety. Anxiety will most certainly lead to lower productivity and may even spoil the result. If we can treat our work effort as a chain of events, it will increase our productivity.

2.14 Dreaming

A small part of our brains replay our daily impressions while we're in rapid eye movement (REM) sleep. That part is called the *hippocampus*, and it's shaped like a seahorse. Memories are stabilized, copied, and filed. The least relevant of the emotional parts are removed. The brain also discovers new relationships between collections of memory. Offline time—when we don't think about a problem—gives us new logical insights. Our brain runs this logical thread in the background, not only while we're asleep but also in offline time when we're awake. Small, regular breaks will improve our deciphering capacity.

Eugène Aserinsky and Nathaniel Kleitman discovered REM sleep in 1953.[12] That was 53 years after Sigmund Freud published his seminal work *Die Traumdeutung.*[13] REM sleep—in other words, *dream sleep*—appears three to five times every night, in periods of five to fifteen minutes, which is a significant part of our lives. In total, we will spend about three years in REM state if we live for 70 years. Non-REM sleep is characterized by slow electrical waves, but during REM sleep, we have similar electrical waves as in the awake state: low amplitude at a rapid pace.[14]

---

12. *Regularly occurring periods of eye motility and concomitant phenomena [AK53]*
13. *The Interpretation of Dreams [Fre80]*
14. *Hjärnans futurum. [Ing01]*

2.15 Absorbing

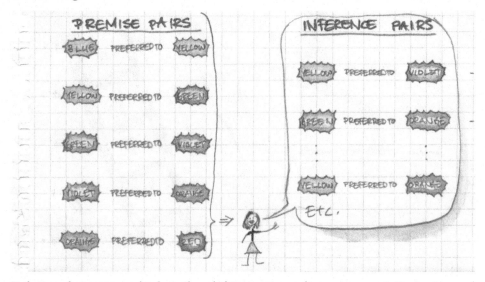

Relational memory, which is the ability to generalize across existing personal knowledge, is highly affected by offline time such as REM sleep or even small (awake) breaks from problem solving. One type of relational learning is transitive inference. For example, we initially learn individual premises; if we hear "Yellow is preferred to green" and "Green is preferred to violet," then without ever explicitly being taught the relationship of yellow to violet, we infer that yellow is preferred to violet.

In 2007 Jeffrey M. Ellenbogen et al. tested separate groups of participants, each having achieved the same level of premise pair training, with varying offline times of 20 minutes, 12 hours, and 24 hours. Participants initially learned five premise pairs, such as "Green is preferred to violet" and "Violet is preferred to orange." They were not informed of the hierarchical structure from which inferences could be made, as in "Green is preferred to orange."

Participants tested after 20 minutes could not answer the inference questions. But those tested after 12 or 24 hours of offline time showed a significant improvement in this relational knowledge, irrespective of whether they had slept in between the training and testing.[15]

This explains why I sometimes come up with a solution after lunch or after a night of sleep!

---

15. *Human relational memory requires time and sleep [EHPT07]*

2.16 Food-and-Sleep Clock

Skalman is a turtle-shaped Swedish cartoon character. His name can be literally translated as "shell man." The most interesting thing about him is not that he wears a yellow hat. It's not that he's a genius with technology, logic, and chemistry, and it's not that he invented almost everything from a space rocket to a self-walking wheelbarrow.

The most remarkable thing about Skalman is his favorite invention: the Food-and-Sleep Clock. Whenever it rings, he must do what it says. Well, he has chosen this lifestyle himself. Either the clock tells him to eat or it tells him to sleep. It doesn't matter whether the monster is just about to devour Skalman and his best friends, Bamse and Lille Skutt. If the clock says it's time to sleep, then Skalman immediately goes to sleep. (Skalman made an exception back in 1982, though; Bamse and his wife, Brummelisa, had triplets, and Skalman skipped a meal.)

This is strictly timeboxed and iterative behavior. He relies on the clock and as a consequence, in contrast to Bamse and Lille Skutt, he's always able to act logically, even under pressure. Recurring gestures and routines help the brain adapt to the context.

2.17 Flow

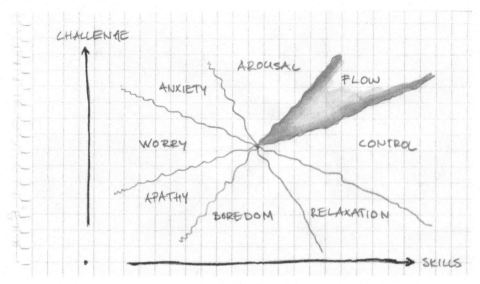

The mental state, characterized by the following properties, is known as *flow*: clear goals, concentration and focus, a loss of the feeling of self-consciousness, a distorted sense of time, direct and immediate feedback, balance between ability level and challenge, a sense of personal control, intrinsically rewarding, the merging of action and awareness.[16]

Flow is a state of creativity. Wouldn't it be highly effective to always have flow? No, it wouldn't. Flow is not compatible with overview. Creativity is not compatible with real control. For example, now and then I want to see the big picture and make strategic decisions about the activity that I will dedicate myself to during my next flow.

Before I enter a flow period, I want to wind up a timer that later wakes me up so that I can temporarily put on my strategy hat and see the big picture. Then I'll go back to flow again—it's rhythm. Also, bear in mind that the prospects for getting into the flow are much better when you are rested, seated, and focused than when you are just hanging around and waiting for inspiration.

---

16. *Flow [Csi02]*

2.18 Arousal

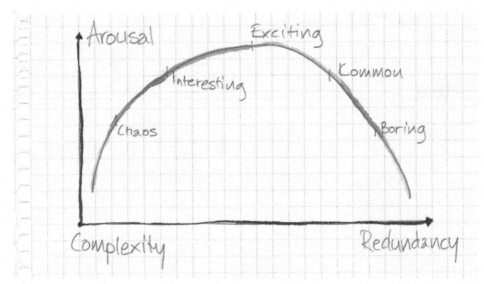

Say I just started a new major activity such as a new project at work. There's a lot of information to gather and analyze, so I have to talk to many people. Even discovering who to talk to is a project in itself. The situation might appear to be chaotic, but in reality it's more like it's complex. Every piece of information is unique, and there's no redundancy. The setup time is long, even before I get started.

As time goes by, I start to see patterns in what used to be a mess. The more I learn, the more interesting the task becomes. At some point, I even become totally excited about it. I can't stop thinking about and working on this activity.

Then, when I know everything about it, it becomes more and more boring. The most important things are done, but I still have to put the finishing touches on it. I have to tidy up and make the result of the activity presentable. Once again, I have a long setup time before I get started.

Arousal is a state of heightened physiological activity. I don't need the peaks, and I definitively don't want the troughs. I want to have a sustainable pace.

2.19 Procrastination

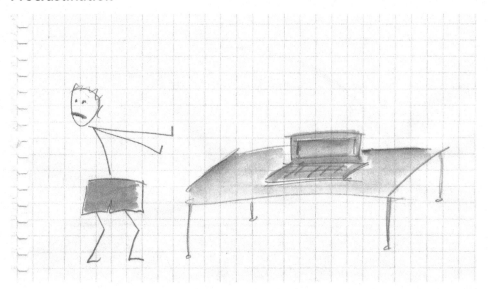

Procrastination is a mechanism for coping with the anxiety associated with starting or completing any task or decision. Why do you procrastinate? Because you're lazy? No, even the worst procrastinator has motivation and energy for something—a weekend hobby, a relationship, or perhaps a community.

There are three outstanding sources of procrastination:

- That other people force you to do something against your will
- Your own pressure for making a perfect performance
- Fear of making mistakes or receiving criticism

Let's say you are chronically late, and deadlines surprise you. You have insufficient time for relationships and recreation. Why? It's because procrastination feels like a reward. It gives you temporary relief from stress. Remember that stress comes from the inside, and the cure is to find a starting point for your project.[17]

---

17. *The Now Habit [Fio07]*

2.20 Heroism and Guilt

Overtime comes from a combination of heroism and guilt. A promise to deliver can create guilt.

Let me tell you a story about undeserved hero status. Once I spent a whole night at the office in order to fix a bug. Before I went home at 4 a.m., I sent an email to the project leader, explaining that the bug was fixed. The next day, the very same project leader fired off emails to the whole division, including all the vice presidents in the company. I was given a hero's reception —not for fixing the bug but for the devotion of being at the office in the middle of the night.

Let's make this clear from the beginning: working overtime is like shopping with a credit card. With it, you buy things you can't afford right now. In the end, you have to pay everything with real money anyway. And—I can't stress this strongly enough—you will have to pay interest for the service of spending more than you can afford right now. It's a short-sighted way of managing time, since the interest charge will slow you down in the future. In the long run, we will produce more if we have a sustainable pace. Our brains need regular recreation time—both short breaks during the workday and long breaks every day from the whole office environment.

2.21 Regulatory Process

I used to travel smoothly in traffic until the day that I got glasses. Now cars emerge from everywhere!

A *regulator* maintains a desired level of a designated characteristic or quality. For example, a thermostat controls the flow of heat energy into or out of a system. Actions taken by the thermostat are based on the feedback from a sensor. The system adapts its behavior, depending on sensor measurements and the desired level. An aircraft is another example that relies on regulatory processes. The autopilot takes the plane long distances even though the weather conditions fluctuate.

So, why shouldn't a methodology be adapted at tight intervals?

Relevant metrics should be tracked seamlessly during focused work. Recurring sessions are earmarked for analyzing the tracked data and also for looking forward: how can we adapt our process to our current office environment, our current type of activities, our current tools, our current teammates, our current deadlines, and all our other current circumstances?

2.22 Thin Slicing

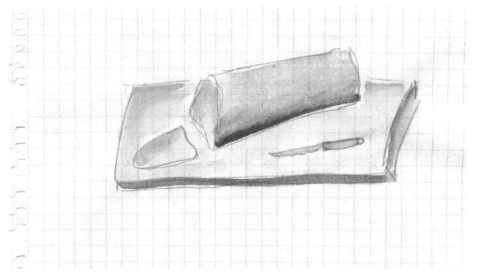

Sometimes I recognize patterns and make conclusions that are based on imaginary facts. My gut feeling tells me to choose one option, but my decision gets corrupted when I over-analyze. I'm interpreting items that I don't understand—with a little help from what I like and dislike, the stereotypes I know, and the rumors that I've heard.

Good decisions balance between awareness and intuition. To make a good decision, you need to simplify the question to consist of only the significant facts and the areas that you're competent enough to analyze. *Thin slicing* is when we think without thinking. We extract what is really important from a slight period of experience. The quality of these judgments comes from our experience, training, and knowledge—nothing else.[18]

It is a true challenge to set up a process that is simple, transparent, supportive, self-improving, and adaptive. The adaptation is based on facts that we track, and these metrics should not only tailor our process but also improve us. We will then be able to make split-second decisions to do the right activity, at the right time, and in the right way.

---

18. *Blink [Gla06]*

2.23 Embrace Change

Suppose that I've been working hard on a high-priority activity for more than a month. Then my boss turns up and tells me that this project is now useless, since the customer who ordered this feature has gone bankrupt. All the work that I've done is now wasted. How could I possibly have known this when I started a month ago? What did I learn? To give and get feedback more often. Then me, my boss, and the customer would have been able to predict this failure earlier.

Change is an ever-present part of business. We can't always control it, but sometimes we can control the effect change has on us. Learning to embrace change will open windows of opportunity and eliminate stress.

It is easy to mistakenly believe that late changes have to be unprofitable; the cost of change always increases exponentially. With this reasoning, we have to plan meticulously in advance to avoid major changes later. But with the good practices, we can often make the cost of change curve flatten: we have control over the activities we must do, and we often reassess by asking "What is most important to complete?" in the long and short term.

If we can force the cost of change to rise only slowly as time passes, we will act completely differently from what we will do if costs rise exponentially. We will make major impact decisions as late in the process as possible to defer the cost of making the decisions and to have the greatest possible chance that they will be right.[19]

---

19. *Extreme Programming Explained: Embrace Change [Bec00]*

2.24 Paradox of Choice

Constantly choosing all the time between all possible alternatives creates anxiety and disturbs our focus. We have too many choices, too many decisions, and too little time to do what is really important. Choosing creates anxiety, and evaluating alternatives steals time and focus.[20]

Still, we want to do the most important thing all the time. When our environment changes in a way that affects the value of what we're currently doing, we should want to embrace this change and perhaps change our priorities.

We must limit the occasions where we're forced to sort or allocate priorities, in other words, choosing our current activity. But, we must have these occasions often enough to be able to react to change, in other words, switching between activities. We need a rhythm such as choosing-working-break, choosing-working-break, and so on. And we need to timebox the work slots so that we won't forget to leave the zone when all our attention is on our current activity.

---

20. *The Paradox of Choice: Why More is Less [Sch05]*

2.25 Self-Reflection on Context

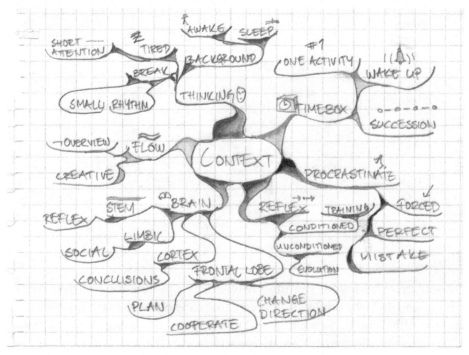

- For how long can you focus on one mentally challenging activity?
- What are the rhythms in your private and your professional life?
- Do you lose when you play games that reward good memory?
- When did you last procrastinate? Why?
- How do you balance between intuitive and conscious decisions?

CHAPTER 3

Mechanics

3.1 A Cucumber and an Artichoke Meet at the Library

Cucumber: *How are you progressing with the Pomodoro Technique?*

Artichoke: *Things are going well. I've implemented the entire process.*

Cucumber: *How do you figure out which activities you should do?*

Artichoke: *Most of the time I just know. I have a good memory.*

Cucumber: *And how do you notice that 25 minutes have passed?*

Artichoke: *I remember the time I started my iteration. But sometimes, of course, I forget to stop.*

Cucumber: *I don't think you have even implemented half the process. There is a more formal way to do the Pomodoro Technique—with kitchen timer, artifacts, and retrospective. It helps you to not forget anything and adapts your process for you every day.*

Artichoke: *Is it complicated?*

Cucumber: *Not at all.*

3.2 Learning the Technique

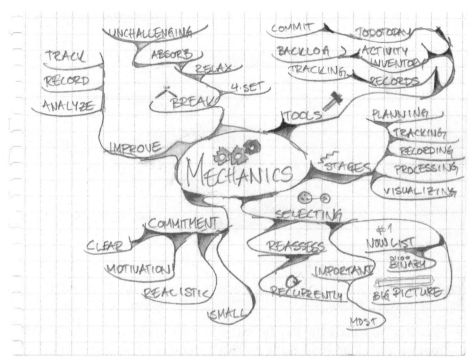

It's simple. Choose the highest-priority activity on the To Do Today sheet, wind up the clock to 25 minutes, and start focusing on that activity—and only that one.

Finally, you have made it to the core practices! This chapter will walk you through the stages, the artifacts, and the how-tos of the Pomodoro Technique. And as you come to the end of this chapter, you will have practiced a complete day including creating your Activity Inventory sheet and your To Do Today sheet.

3.3   Stages

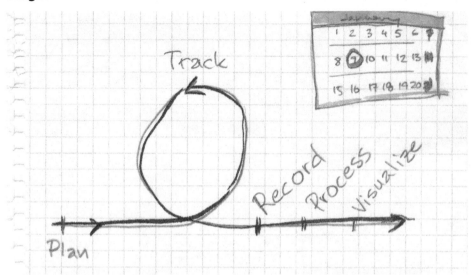

Here's a quick look at a day with the Pomodoro Technique. These are the five stages that you'll follow.

- *Planning*: You start the day by extracting the most important activities from your backlog—called the Activity Inventory—and writing them in a list on your To Do Today sheet. This is your commitment for the day.
- *Tracking*: Once you've decided on your activities for the day, you wind up the timer for 25 minutes and then start in on the first one. During every 25-minute timebox—called a *Pomodoro*—you collect a small amount of process metrics. You may, for example, count the number of times that you get interrupted.
- *Recording*: At the end of the day, you file your daily observations on the Records sheet. If you tracked the number of interruptions, then this number is saved here.
- *Processing*: After recording, you convert the raw data into information. For example, you might calculate how many interruptions you get in an average 25-minute timebox.
- *Visualizing*: Finally, you organize the information in a way that helps you see how to improve your process. This is basically a daily retrospective and when you acclimatize your working habits to your reality.

Every day starts with the Planning stage and ends with Recording, Processing, and Visualizing stages. In between, there is an iterative loop of 25-minute Tracking sessions.

3.4   Deming-Shewhart Cycle

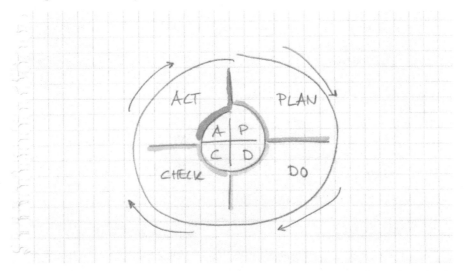

The American statistician William Edwards Deming, along with Andrew Walter Shewhart, invented PDCA (Plan-Do-Check-Act). It's an iterative problem-solving process that can be used to improve other processes, and it is based on the scientific method Hypothesis-Experiment-Evaluation, which represents Plan-Do-Check-Act.

- *Plan*: You define your goals and the processes you need to deliver the expected results.
- *Do*: You implement the new process.
- *Check*: You measure the new process and compare the results to the expected outcome in order to find discrepancies.
- *Act*: You analyze the discrepancies and try to understand the root cause of them.

This particular type of planning, monitoring, measuring, and improving is also the core of the Pomodoro Technique—and it makes it a typical PDCA process. In the morning, decide which tasks to do and what to track. You then track events throughout the day in the form of Xs, apostrophes, dashes, and other symbols of your choice. At the end of the day, compare your tracked data with tracked data from recent days and the expectations that you had beforehand. Did you manage to complete the activities that you committed to on your To Do Today this morning? Then think about how you can improve the process for tomorrow. Repeat this cycle every day to improve your process iteratively.[1]

---

1.   *5s Kaizen [Fre08]*

3.5 Tools

Tools that are easy to use make a method less complicated. You can then concentrate on the real tasks and ignore the process mechanics. In the Pomodoro Technique, you merely need a pen or pencil, a kitchen timer, and three plain sheets of paper.

You can use whatever type of timer works for your office circumstances. It could be a mechanical kitchen timer, a digital kitchen timer, an hourglass, a mobile phone possibly set to vibrate, or some software on your computer. The act of winding up a mechanical clock will tutor your conditioned reflexes. After a while, this behavior will support your rhythm.

The three pieces of paper that you'll need for the Pomodoro Technique are the following:

- The *To Do Today sheet* is a paper with today's date, your name, and a list of your activities planned for today. You create a new one every morning.

- The *Activity Inventory sheet* holds your name and an unsorted list of your upcoming activities in the near future. You use the same Activity Inventory sheet day after day—adding new activities and crossing out completed ones.

- The *Records sheet* is where you keep your sampled process metrics to be used for your process improvement. The same Records sheet is used day after day—in order to compare today's tracking with prior tracking.

3.6   Try It Now: Make an Activity Inventory Sheet

Bookmark this page, and go get a pen, a piece of paper, and your kitchen timer. Wind up the clock for five minutes. Write the header "Activity Inventory" at the top of the sheet and start to think about activities you need to do at home. Write down all of them, whether they are important or not. Do not worry about order or priority. Don't write what to do. Write how things will be when the activity is completed. For example:

1. Living room tidy

2. Cookbook ordered

3. Thea emailed

Don't use abbreviations or long descriptions—just write the important words. You don't need to write so that other people can understand. What matters is that you understand your own activity titles, even if you write them today and read them in a month. It's easier if the activity's first word is a topic area —something that may reappear on several titles—and the second word is more specifically what you want to achieve.

Write the activities in a vertical list; one on each line. You can also write down when they must be done by, if you know that. If you're having a dinner party at 7 p.m. that night, you might write "Living room tidy, 7 p.m." And do not stop this exercise until the clock rings. Then continue to read this book.

3.7 Finding the Starting Point

Without the Pomodoro Technique, figuring out how to start each workday can be hard. You might feel like you have a billion things and you can't possibly do everything simultaneously. So, you never really start, and suddenly it's lunch time.

The concept of "do it now" is a good principle for reducing the total amount of work you have to do. For example, as an independent software development consultant, I manage my own company. This entails all my regular work and also mandatory paperwork such as keeping the books, sending invoices, and filling in tax forms. Postponing this work makes it even harder and more complicated because I can forget important details as time passes. To wait for inspiration is a bad thing.

For me, keeping a long to-do list is not enough because it's a question of selectivity. At the moment I decide to do one activity, I'm also implicitly deciding *not* to do the other hundreds of possible activities residing in my backlog.[2]

First prioritizing and then focusing on the most important activity will make you feel safe and sound. Otherwise, your focus will constantly be disturbed by questions like "Am I really doing the most important thing now?" At the start of my day, for instance, I first look at the whole backlog and pick the most important activity. Then I stick to it for a short timebox, before I

---

2. *Get Everything Done* [For00]

reevaluate whether it's still the most important one. In my mind I replace "I must finish" with "Where can I start?" and I replace "This project is so big and important" with "I can take one small step".[3]

3.8 Morning

With the Pomodoro Technique, it's not hard to know where to start. Let me show you how I do it. At the start of my Pomodoro Technique day, I select the most important activities from the Activity Inventory sheet and write them in a list on my To Do Today sheet. This is the Planning stage.

Then I choose the highest-priority activity on the To Do Today sheet, wind up the clock to 25 minutes, and start focusing on that activity—and only that one. In my head, I say that this activity is on the "now list." This virtual list is actually binary. It holds either one or no activity.

Being able to do something because you have decided to do it is the foundation of good time management. You need to see the big picture when you decide what to do; otherwise, you will be bogged down with trivia. Every morning with the Pomodoro Technique, you can see all the activities available and choose a selection from them.[4]

The Pomodoro Technique is very goal-oriented. You select only the number of activities that you realistically stand a chance of completing today. This is your commitment. If you manage to complete them all, you get rewarded with a mental trophy.

---

3. *The Now Habit [Fio07]*
4. *Get Everything Done [For00]*

3.9   Try It Now: Make a To Do Today Sheet

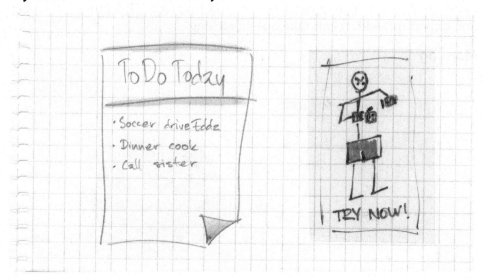

Get a pen, a piece of paper, your kitchen timer, and the Activity Inventory sheet that you just created. Wind up the clock to five minutes. Write the header "To Do Today" at the top of the sheet, and start to think about activities you believe you'll do during the rest of this day.

Look first at your Activity Inventory sheet. Consider whether there are items that you have not entered there. For example:

- Soccer drive Edda

- Dinner cook

- Call sister

Do not write too many things without thinking about whether it is a reasonable commitment to complete all activities. Do not stop this exercise until the clock rings. Then continue to read from here.

How would you feel if you got all these activities done today? Selecting activities for To Do Today sheet also means that you refuse all activities that you don't write down on this list. Is it easier to focus on the selected activities now?

3.10 Commitment

A traditional to-do list is not a commitment. It may feel safe to add every potential activity there, including things that other people push on you. The list is long, and the continuous inward flow ensures that all activities can't possibly ever be done. Without commitment, there is less motivation. It's not really an achievement to complete and remove one line from this inventory that is still enormous.

Your To Do Today sheet is your timeboxed commitment. You shouldn't put activities there that you do not think you will do today. This sheet allows you to see a goal that is reasonable to reach that very day. By contrast, the Activity Inventory sheet is a more traditional to-do list. It's allowed to grow, and you can put nice-to-haves there, even if you're not sure that they will ever be a high enough priority to be executed.

Let me stress that an Activity Inventory sheet is a good thing. But it's not enough. To develop motivation, you need to extract an activity set from the inventory that is adequate for a timebox that you can foresee. If you extract this set yourself and you believe that it's an attainable goal within the timebox, then you will be committed. One day is a foreseeable timebox length, and it's also long enough to complete activities in every commitment.

Distinguishing between the Activity Inventory (a traditional to-do list) and the To Do Today (an extracted commitment) is a compulsory strategy for doing the right thing, getting started now, and putting optimum effort into your work. It gives you clear goals and personal control.

3.11 Direct and Immediate Feedback

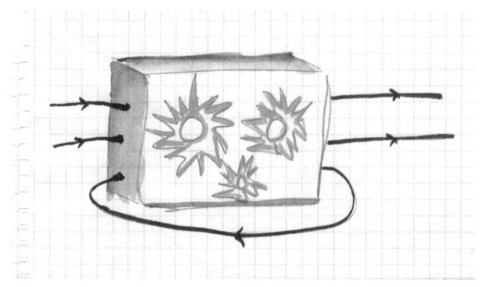

When people go bowling, they have a clear goal. They must roll the ball down the lane with the objective of knocking down as many pins as possible. Every time they do this, they know immediately whether they did it well or not. How many pins is not interesting in itself, but it's interesting in a context. What will be the consequences now that I've knocked down six pins? How will that affect my next step? Humans get satisfaction when our investment of mental energy—our attention—results in success.[5]

For example, when I'm working on an activity for days and weeks, I never get this type of direct and immediate feedback. Successes and failures will not be apparent until the big task is done. If the activity I'm doing has a deadline some days from now, it will be even worse. The uncertainty about whether I will manage to meet the deadline will give me anxiety.

With the Pomodoro Technique, rating 25 minutes of effort as a success gives us immediate feedback.

5.   *Flow [Csi02]*

3.12 Prospective Memory

To avoid focusing on less important activities, you need to remember to recurrently reassess which activity is most important. You also have to remember to frequently take breaks. And you must remember to now and then do a personal introspection to improve your abilities and to be aware of your weaknesses. For me, I support my prospective memory with a written plan, a solid process, and a ring signal that I have programmed.

People's *retrospective* memory is concerned about the past. The complement is our *prospective* memories, which is what helps us remember to do something in the future. For example, we use our prospective memories when we remember to attend a meeting, remember to call someone, or more generally remember to perform any kind of activity that we, in the past, intended to do in the future.

Aging decreases the activity in our frontal lobes and our production of prospective memories. This is a fact of life, but we can compensate by external stimuli, such as creating reminders for ourselves. Prospective memories are closely connected to our wills. For example, if we want things to happen in the future, we create long-term plans. And when those plans are accomplished, we're rewarded.[6]

---

6. *Hjärnans futurum [Ing01]*

3.13 The Now List

In 1933 Hedwig von Restorff performed a set of memory experiments. Her conclusion was that a visually isolated item, in a list of otherwise similar items, would be better remembered. For example, if you read a shopping list with one item highlighted in azure blue, it's more likely that you'll remember the highlighted item than any of the others. This is now identified as the Von Restorff effect.

The "now list" is not another tangible artifact in the Pomodoro Technique process. It's my name for a concept—the thing that I'm giving my attention to right now. The cardinality of my "now list" is binary. I focus on either one activity or zero activities. It can never be two, three, four, or any other number of activities. Before I wind up the clock, I choose one single activity. My challenge during a 25-minute Pomodoro is to not give another activity any attention.

The Von Restorff effect tells us that we can provoke our memories to store things that we highlight. So, to apply that effect to my "now list," I explicitly write the current activity that I'm doing on a slip of paper and put it in front of me. Or, to apply the technique even more literally, I may use a highlighter felt-tip pen to mark the current activity on the To Do Today sheet and then later cross the item off with a black pen when I complete the activity.

3.14 Break

When your kitchen timer rings after 25 minutes, it means you have completed one Pomodoro. You should immediately mark an X next to the activity on your To Do Today sheet and then take a break. Your break period can vary, but I totally detach myself for three to five minutes from the activity and everything else that is mentally challenging. I might drink water or think about what to eat for dinner that night.

My minimum criterion for a break is to stand and move at least two steps from my office chair. That usually washes away my thoughts about the previous Pomodoro and also does some good to my back and shoulders. Office people like us sit for far too long in monotonous positions.

After your break, you should decide whether to continue with the same activity or switch to another one. A switch could be initiated either by a change in priorities or otherwise by the simple fact you have completed the last activity.

3.15 Detach

During your breaks, you're not allowed to think about the previous Pomodoro or about the next Pomodoro. Don't make important phone calls or start writing important emails. Your brain needs to absorb the last 25 minutes of challenging thinking.

If your stress system is never neutralized by mental recreation, you'll notice a number of symptoms. The thinking system in the brain stem is affected, as well as the senses of the limbic system and in the end your biological rhythms. For example, your sleep might be affected.

At chronic stress levels, the capacity of your working memory and your ability to concentrate will fall. The joy of working will be transformed into anxiety—inspiration is altered to irritation.[7]

---

7. *Blink [Gla06]*

3.16 Set Break

In addition to the breaks you take after each timeboxed iteration, the Pomodoro Technique includes a *set break*, which is bit longer than a regular break. For me, four Pomodori makes a Pomodoro set, so after every four Pomodori, I take my set break. Typically, a set break is 15 to 30 minutes of recreation. You can use this time to clean your desk, take a walk to the coffee machine, or browse your favorite community on the Web.

You can even glance at your email inbox. But don't start to write any important replies. That task should be scheduled like all the other activities.

Since people are naturally inquisitive, you might want small activities. You can see the goal already from the beginning, and you're more likely to see small activities as a commitment. If you intersperse short periods of work with breaks and rewards, it will give you the motivation to keep a sustainable pace through the day, and day after day.

These breaks are an example of guilt-free play. During your break, you will know that you already have achieved goals during the recent Pomodoro. And what's more, you'll get insights throughout the day, even during a break.[8]

How to Take a Five-Minute Nap
by: Renzo Borgatti

The Pomodoro Technique advocates a 25-minute slot of quality, focused work followed by a five-minute break. There are so many ways to spend the break time, but the main goal is to

---

8. *The Now Habit [Fio07]*

recharge the brain and allow for background processing of previously assimilated information. The consequence is that you shouldn't be tempted to spend the break reading emails, reading the news, making phone calls, or doing anything that generates additional pressure to the following Pomodoro.

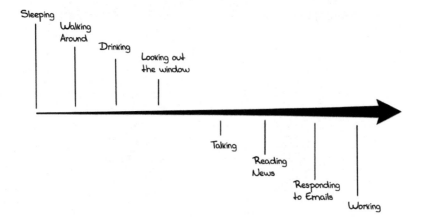

So, for example, looking at the previous picture, I can say that looking out the window requires less effort than talking or reading emails. At the extremes are sleeping and working. Focused, quality work is the goal of the Pomodoro, and a focused, quality relaxation is the goal of the break. I made the mistake of thinking that just looking at email subjects or news titles was relaxing enough for a break, but after comparing it with five minutes of deep relaxation, I changed my mind.

Ideally, the goal of the break should be light sleep for five minutes. I don't know if it's possible to sleep for just five minutes, but you can train yourself to really relax. After a couple of weeks of self-inspection of the break and implementing some relaxing techniques, I can say I'm very happy with the results. I discovered that a good-quality five-minute break can immediately give me the energy to start the next Pomodoro with unexpected ease.

The problem is how to quickly fall into deep relaxation. I had success with the following:

1. Find a comfy chair or, if you happen to have one at work, a couch.
2. As soon as the break starts, close your eyes and find the best relaxing position. Your neck, arms, and legs should be perfectly relaxed.
3. Think about a light scanner—a horizontal line of light starting from your head and going down to your feet very slowly. While the line of light touches all your muscles, concentrate on that single area and further relax whatever is there. Especially important are the eyes: carefully remove tenseness.
4. Think about a white giant rectangle gently floating around. If that disappears, no big deal. It's just a starter thought to get you distracted from thinking about the goal of the previous Pomodoro.
5. When the break is done, gently open your eyes, start the Pomodoro, focus, and go.

You know that you're doing it correctly if those five minutes feel like ten. Every time I failed to properly relax, I paid the consequences after five to six Pomodori. Something I also tried was to sleep during the 20-minute or longer breaks. That was real sleep, but it was never too deep to be counterproductive. Needless to say, the long break is as important as the shorter ones for a good day of Pomodori.

The technique works well in environments with low noise that are familiar (where people don't pay too much attention to you). I borrowed the idea to train the body to deeply sleep in short period of times from the polyphasic sleep model, a fascinating (and scary) way to sleep less.[9]

3.17 Itinerary

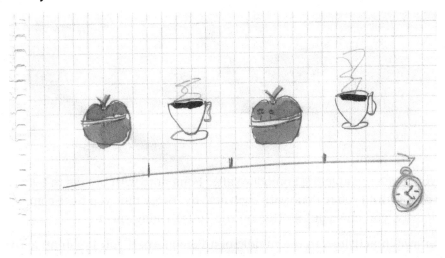

Free time is fuel for the working brain. I never spend five minutes extra on an activity when the clock rings. If I did, it would slow me down for the next Pomodoro. When the clock rings, I finish the word I'm writing and maybe put a memo tag on a scrap paper—just to remember the direction that my mind was going in.

An itinerary sets limits. In the Planning stage, you have essentially designed your itinerary for today's journey. It doesn't mean that you can't consider new facts and replan. Schedule updates have to be done in a mind state of overview and not in the state of flow. Also, you can make more aware decisions when you're rested after a short break than immediately after a long period of deep concentration.

For me, concrete goals motivate me to complete things. Selecting a realistic number of activities in the morning is my commitment. Trying to meet the commitment in small iterations—my Pomodoro—is my itinerary. Paying no heed to breaks will spoil everything including the commitment and motivation. Respecting the itinerary gives me unwavering productivity all the time.

---

9.   http://en.wikipedia.org/wiki/Polyphasic

3.18 Activity Completed

So, you're now completing Pomodoro after Pomodoro with breaks in between. You do this until you're done with each activity. Every time you have completed an activity, you cross out its title on the To Do Today sheet.

Never switch activities in the middle of a Pomodoro. If you finish an activity halfway through a Pomodoro, spend the rest of the time over-learning. For example, if I finish early, I review what I have done, I repeat what I have learned, I see whether I can enhance my work, or I note new conclusions on paper—until the kitchen timer rings.

Over-learning is when we continue to study or practice even after attaining proficiency. Malcolm Gladwell argues that this is necessary if we want to be really good at something: "Once a musician has enough ability to get into a top music school, the thing that distinguishes one performer from another is how hard he or she works. That's it. And what's more, the people at the very top don't work just harder or even much harder than everyone else. They work much, much harder.".[10]

So, you're not allowed to impulsively switch activities in the middle of a Pomodoro. In fact, just having the option to switch in the middle is a recurring disturbance. You can't just stop in the middle of a Pomodoro and take a break either. Then you will lose the rhythm. And since the stopped Pomodoro was shorter, it will not be compatible—in terms of tracking—with other Pomodori.

---

10. *Outliers: The Story of Success [Gla08]*

3.19 Abstract Time Unit

When you don't use the Pomodoro Technique, you have many tasks to do, and your teammates or your client wants to know when you're going to be done with them. Often that creates problems.

Predicting how long something will take and then realizing that your guess is counted as a promise creates anxiety. The problem is that you don't know exactly how long the activity will take, and you will be punished—by, for example, missing a client's expectations—if you don't live up to your prediction. Anxiety reduces motivation and productivity.

As you know, in the Pomodoro Technique, a single Pomodoro is 25 minutes of effort. It's an indivisible and abstract unit—a timebox that disregards scope. Basically, you promise to spend 25 minutes of effort in the best possible way that you can. Whether the activity is completed during this iteration is not an issue while you're in the Pomodoro. The only thing that counts at that moment is that you do your best.

How does this help you tell your client or your teammates when you'll be done with an activity? Actually, it doesn't. But, when you're in a Pomodoro, you should only care about the 25 minutes—not about when the whole activity is completed. This will help you focus.

The clock is visible, and it counts down from 25 to 0. After 25 minutes, you get the intrinsic reward. You write an X and take a break with guilt-free playing.[11] This gives you the feeling, throughout the Pomodoro, that you're getting closer and closer to a reward.

---

11. *The Now Habit [Fio07]*

3.20 Recording and Processing

Once your working day is about to end, you enter the Recording stage. To start, copy your raw tracking data to your Records sheet.

What you track depends on what you want to see. When you start with the Pomodoro Technique, it's good to just track the number of Pomodori that you have completed during the day. So, you make one column with today's date and one with today's number of completed Pomodori. You keep the Records sheet day after day, and each line represents one day.

Tracking data can answer questions about the way you work and help you improve your productivity. Why do I put so much effort into my work and get so few activities done? It could be because I achieve so few 25-minute time-boxes. Is this bad or is this good? Perhaps it's good, because I'm supposed to spend a major amount of my time helping other people. Anyway, now I have an explanation that is empirical and correct.

After the Recording stage comes the Processing stage. This is where you turn the abstract data into informative bits. For example, you could calculate the average amount of Pomodori spent on one activity. If this is a massive number, you will learn to break down the activities into smaller and more manageable pieces. Or you can measure the average time an activity stays on the Activity Inventory sheet before you handle it. The calculated numbers are also on the Records sheet.

3.21 Try It Now: Recording

Get a pen, a piece of paper, your kitchen timer, and your calendar. Bookmark this page, and wind up the clock for three minutes. Write the header "Records" at the top of the sheet.

Look at how many items you have in the calendar that were scheduled for yesterday. Did you have any meetings in the office, for example? Enter yesterday's date and to the right of this the number of items that were on it yesterday. On the next row, do the same thing for the day before yesterday. Continue backward in time until the clock rings. Then return to reading this book.

Look at your Records sheet, and figure out how many items you have on average per day. Is the sum greater or less than you thought? Should you have more or fewer entries in the calendar?

3.22 Kaizen

This Japanese word *Kaizen* means "to change over time for that which is better." But it's more commonly translated as "continuous improvement." Kaizen is an approach to work that focuses on incremental changes aiming for improvement. For example, maintaining cleanliness should be part of your daily work. And you should be answering these questions every day: Do I need smaller activities? Am I bothered by a recurring distraction? Do I have unnecessary overhead in my standardized activities and personal process?

Doing the improvement work in a scientific way helps me remember to do it. First I standardize a practice. Then I measure the standardized practice in some way. Then I compare the metrics to the requirements. Maybe I have to change how I work to meet the requirements. Then I measure again, and finally I standardize the new, improved way of working.

An example: I decide to work in 40-minute iterations. Then I measure how many iterations I can complete in a day. Finally, I compare that number with my expectations. I realize that I completed too few iterations, so I decide to decrease the iteration size to 25 minutes.

Recording tracking data and analyzing it in the end of every day is *self-centered observation*. Improving your practices, based on this analysis, is *incremental upgrading*.[12]

---

12. *5s Kaizen [Fre08]*

3.23 Right Here, Right Now

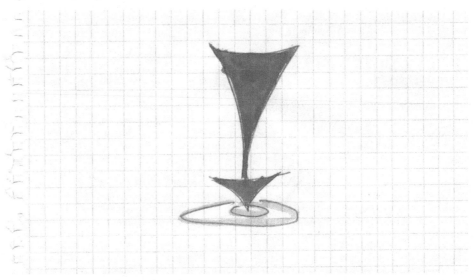

The Pomodoro Technique has a regulatory nature. Every failure can be transformed into an insight. The retrospective at the end of the day is a deliberate time and place to customize your personal process. For me, I want suitable habits for my current type of activities, office, teammates, and every other possible boundary around me.

The small iterations and the daily commitment shrink what's important for me at this moment. While in a Pomodoro, I don't care about the future or about the past. There's time to reflect on the big picture when you are planning in the morning, when allocating priorities before every Pomodoro, and when recording, processing, and visualizing at the end of the day.

It's one daily commitment—one Pomodoro, one activity, and one goal.

3.24 Self-Reflection on Mechanics

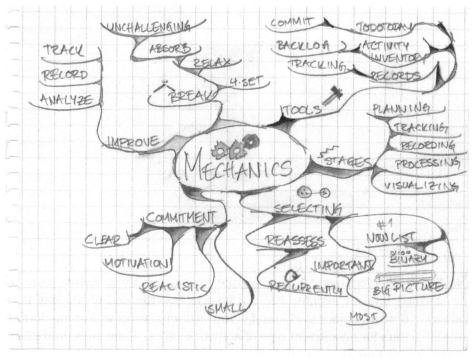

- Have you ever experienced drawbacks with a long to-do list?

- What makes you feel mentally rewarded?

- What type of timer is right for you?

- How often do you take a break at work?

- When do you scrutinize your work habits?

CHAPTER 4

Interruptions

4.1 A Cucumber and an Artichoke Speak on the Phone

Cucumber: *Hi Artie! See you at the bar tonight?*

Artichoke: *Maybe. It depends a bit on...*

Cucumber: *Depends on what?*

Artichoke: *Wait a minute, I just got an email...*

Cucumber: *We can go there another day.*

Artichoke: *Today is a great day to go to the bar, provided that...*

Cucumber: *What?*

Artichoke: *Got my copy?*

Cucumber: *What copy?*

Artichoke: *Sorry, Artie. I was talking to a guy here in the office. You asked me something?*

Cucumber: *Nah, I just wondered what's the weather like over there. I'll call again tomorrow.*

Artichoke: *OK! Always nice to talk to you.*

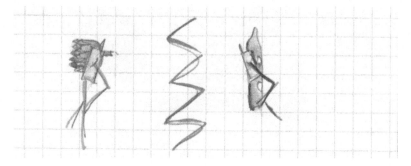

4.2 Keeping on Course

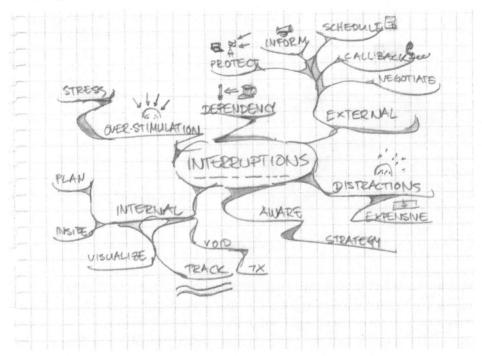

Email and phone are easy—you can turn them off.

You have now learned that you should neither switch activities nor stop an activity in the middle of a Pomodoro. What about interruptions outside of your control? You get a phone call, you remember some urgent activity you need to do, or you desperately need to visit the restroom. The Pomodoro Technique can't protect us from all kinds of interruptions. But in this chapter, you'll learn how you can handle them in a rational and effective way.

4.3   Attention Deficit Trait

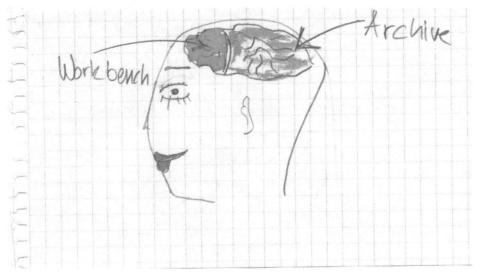

American research has shown that office employees are interrupted approximately every third minute and that people who work in front of a computer screen have an average of eight windows open simultaneously. Psychiatrist Edward Hallowell coined the term *attention deficit trait* (ADT) to describe this severe way of modern life. The brain is inundated with a torrent of information that never runs dry.

Imagine you're starting your day sorting new emails when the IT department calls and urges you to fill in some form at once? Then a colleague steps in to your room and asks a work-related question, and at the same time someone calls you and needs information on the spot to prepare for a meeting?

New findings in psychology and brain research point to the same bottleneck for both simultaneous capacity and handling distractions: the limitation of the working memory. Every distraction makes us lose the original information that we had on our brain workbench. And when attention is lost, it's expensive to find it again.[1]

---

1.   *The Overflowing Brain [Kli08]*

4.4 Avoid LIFO and BPUF

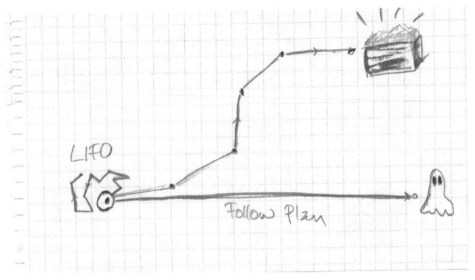

Interruptions are constant. New requests come up all the time. If you always try to meet the last-known need, all your long-term activities end up taking a backseat. You will never finish anything, since the last thing that came in will be first to come out—Last-In-First-Out (LIFO). Add to this the inability to complete activities, since you have to put so much energy into the process of constantly receiving and evaluating new information. This will lead you to a state of chronic mental over-stimulation. It will increase your stress level and affect your results.

One alternative to LIFO is to make a Big Plan Up Front (BPUF). You sit down on New Year's Eve with a pen and a piece of paper. First you write down what to do January 1. Then you go ahead and plan January 2, 3, 4, and so on, until December 31. After that, you buy loads and loads of tinned food, lock yourself in the basement, and start to work for one year. Is this denial of the change around you the way to go? Of courseit's not!

There's a third option out there. It embraces change, it gives you time to focus on your commitments, and it's iterative! It's described on the next page.

4.5   Sustainable Pace

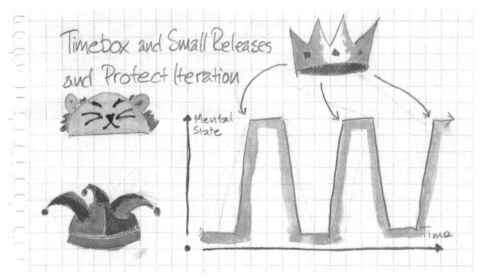

Overview and control are the opposite of flow and deep creative-thinking processes. You can't see the big picture and focus on details at the same time. Your focus will benefit from a process where you minimize the points where you have to sort and allocate priorities. But you need to do both. And you also need recreation time on a regular basis in order to absorb and recharge. So, you have three mental states to switch between. You alternate between them, but what triggers the mental state change?

I use three hats: the recreation hat, which is a jester's hat; the working hat, which transforms me into the lion who is 100 percent focused on hunting the antelope; and the strategy hat, which makes me feel like a king when I'm sorting and deciding what to do during the next work iteration.

I come to work wearing the recreation hat. I put on the strategy hat and choose what activity to focus on. Then I put on the work hat, wind up the clock, and begin to focus. The clock rings after 25 minutes, which reminds me to put on the recreation hat. After a short break, I put on the strategy hat, and so on.

This timebox schedule that interleaves to focus, to prioritize, and to rest gives me a sustainable pace.

4.6   Interruption Strategy

Even though a Pomodoro lasts for only 25 minutes, distractions will still occur. They interrupt us when we're focused and force us to use expensive context switching. Still, the Pomodoro Technique is not a method that suits only lone wolves who can't be team players. Rather, it develops your personal skills in a collaborative environment.

If you have a strategy for handling interruptions, it can cut down on the number of them. Sometimes this strategy will help you carry on with your initial activity, and sometimes it won't.

Interruptions during a Pomodoro come in two flavors.

- First, internal interruptions come from the inside. To elaborate, your instincts send signals to your mind. They tell you to do other things than the activity that you're focused on.

- Second, external interruptions are initiated by someone else. Someone requests something and is waiting for your response.

The Pomodoro Technique has strategies for both these types of interruptions that are covered in the following sections.

4.7 Internal Interruptions

Even though 25 minutes is a small amount of time, it's almost impossible for the Pomodoro Technique practitioner to not think of other important tasks to do, especially in the beginning. But, things that can seem extremely necessary at the moment might not be so significant when everything is summarized.

Here's a typical Pomodoro for me: I wind up the clock and start to focus on one activity. Then I feel hungry. Then I realize I need to make an important call. And I also was just thinking that I want to check my favorite Internet community. And I must read my email and also reply immediately. And that's not to mention the most recurring of all my instincts—refilling my coffee cup whenever it is empty.

All these are instincts that come from inside. I start them, and they are clear symptoms of procrastination. Perhaps I think that my current activity is too complex or redundant. Perhaps I fear upcoming blame for not getting enough quality in my result. Or perhaps I don't want to start before I know exactly how this whole activity will end. Anyway, the interruptions impede me from completing my Pomodoro and writing an X. The next section covers how to get these interruptions under control.

4.8 Accept, Record, and Continue

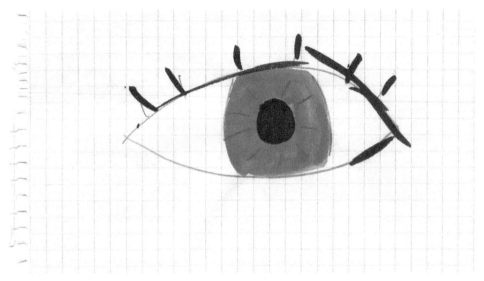

Say during a Pomodoro that I suddenly realize that I need to call the box office. I promised my wife I would reserve tickets for Tchaikovsky's *Nutcracker Suite*. Do I grab the phone and call immediately? No! I follow my process—the Pomodoro Technique. If I want to cut down on interruptions, I first need to have the facts—the real facts. How many interruptions do I get during a day, and what type are they? My interruptions must be visible.

Instead of calling the box office, I write "call box office" on the bottom of my To Do Today sheet. Actually, I have a header in the middle of this sheet, just below my planned commitment, which says Unplanned & Urgent. Calling the box office was totally unplanned, and it seems pretty urgent.

Then I put a small apostrophe in the right margin of the line where my current activity is written on the To Do Today sheet. Writing the apostrophe is essentially tracking. It represents one internal interruption. At the end of the day I can count the number of apostrophes and reflect. This number is a cold hard fact of how many interruptions I had, not just a hectic feeling of forgetting something. Finally, I intensify my determination to finish the current Pomodoro.

So, to reiterate, the strategy when you get an internal interruption is to first accept it, then record it, and then immediately continue with what you were doing before you got interrupted. As for coffee, I allow myself to drink as much coffee as I'd like during a Pomodoro, but I only make or get more coffee during a break between Pomodori.

4.9   Inverting Dependency

The best strategy for dealing with internal interruptions is to observe, accept, and plan or remove. As mentioned, never switch activities in the middle of a Pomodoro. The rule says, "Once a Pomodoro begins, it has to ring." For instance, following my instincts can appear urgent, but with a little distance I realize that the box office will still be ready to answer my call if I choose to do it during my next Pomodoro, instead of interrupting my current one.

Without this strategy, the result of my activities depends on me not responding urgently to any instincts. Now, when I think of something I need to do, I write it down and can then drop it from my mind. I can later schedule it for the next Pomodoro or another day. In other words, the call to the box office can now be put into my schedule and dropped from my mind. What I suddenly and instinctively wanted to do now depends on my schedule. I have "inverted" the dependency.

By the way, if I know from the beginning that I won't call the box office today, I can write it directly on my Activity Inventory sheet and also add a small *u* (unplanned) and a deadline.

4.10 It's Atomic

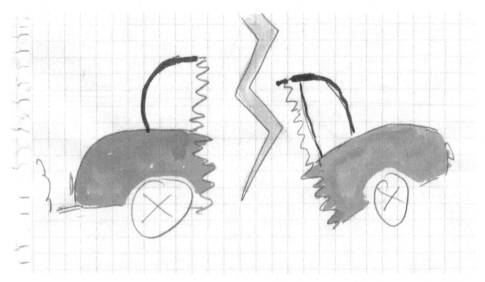

Some internal interruptions can't be fought. If you really have to visit the restroom, then you have to do that. If you glance at the clock before leaving and see that there is 10 minutes left of your Pomodoro, can you then complete the final minutes when you're back from the bathroom? No way.

A Pomodoro is atomic. It's indivisible. It's the smallest monetary unit in this process. If you leave the activity—temporarily or not—then you have to void this Pomodoro. It will not count, and accordingly you're not allowed to write the X. Instead, you wind up the clock 25 minutes and start a new Pomodoro, conceivably preceded by a small break if you think you need that.

Why can't you build a Pomodoro from the sum of small time slots? Because then you will lose the whole idea of rhythm, and it will be too easy to fall for the temptation of interruption. Is it a failure to void a Pomodoro? No, it isn't. The number of completed Pomodori is not an all-purpose measure of competence. It's a measure of the 25-minute atoms of effort you have completed, and it's a fact that can be used to improve your process for tomorrow's work.

4.11 Constant Internal Interruptions

New practitioners of the Pomodoro Technique are surprised of how few Pomodoro they actually complete in one day. Starting to cheat and ignoring that you had internal interruptions is not a solution. The tracking is there for you to improve yourself and your process. It's not to be shown to your boss during your annual salary negotiation.

First, shrink the Pomodoro. Try 15, 10, or even 5 minutes. When you find that you are writing a respectable amount of Xs every day, you can start to expand to 20 and finally 25 minutes at a time. Remember, though, that Pomodori of different length are not compatible. Your tracking will be useless if one X means 5 minutes and another one means 25 minutes. You should go for the smaller Pomodoro for at least two weeks.

You can also track how long it takes until your first internal interruption in every Pomodoro. Try to stay focused just a little bit longer than the last Pomodoro. This tracking can also give you an idea of how long your Pomodori should be in order to avoid being interrupted.

4.12 External Interruptions

In addition to internal interruptions, there are also external interruptions in our lives. These are things like when a colleague drops in and asks you a work-related question. Or when someone drops by to ask you a more social question like, "What did you think about last night's episode of *Curb Your Enthusiasm*?" Or perhaps an old friend calls and wants to talk about old times. Or maybe your project leader needs some estimates from you for her upstream report. Or, the most common one—your email client constantly beeps.

All these interruptions tend to happen while you're trying to focus on an activity in the middle of a Pomodoro! But, if you live in the river, you should make friends with the crocodile. Without understanding the finer nuances, external interruptions will just be irritating.

External interruptions have an interactive nature. Someone is waiting for your response. They are trying to prevent you from writing your X. So, you need a strategy to cut down on interruptions. Still, I can't stress enough that the Pomodoro Technique is not about refusing to help your team buddies. It's not a method for the last man left on the moon.

4.13 Protect the Pomodoro

External interruptions compete for your attention. You need to protect your Pomodoro to focus on completing a commitment. This is the commitment of focusing on one activity for 25 minutes. But when someone comes by your cubicle to see how you liked the latest episode of your favorite TV show, the optimum strategy might not always be to say, "Sorry, I'm in the middle of a Pomodoro. Can you come back later?"

So, you must "invert" the dependency between the Pomodoro and the interruptions. Email and phone are easy—you can turn them off. No one takes for granted that they will get an email reply in less than 25 minutes. Throwing a glance at new email headers (not reading the whole email and definitively not replying) every half an hour just before putting your strategy hat on is more than enough. And voicemail works the same way—as long as you do call back. Sending an email response and calling back should of course be scheduled as an activity and not be handled during a break.

When you get a face-to-face request, ask how long you can defer the activity without reducing the value of your result. It might not matter to the colleague if you offer your response today or on Friday. Then you can suggest the latest possible time to him. Rescheduling interruptions in a later Pomodoro instead of handling them straightaway is a vast benefit.

4.14 Visualize and Then Intensify

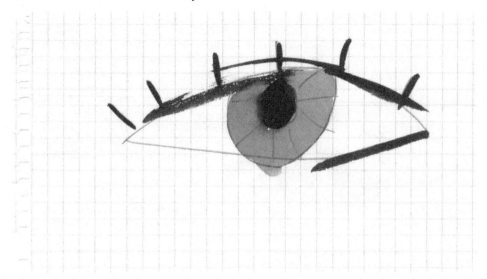

External interruptions must be visible. If you are to cut down on interruptions, you first need to have facts about the type and quantity of your interruptions.

Each time you get an external interruption, reach for your To Do Today sheet, and write down a title for the activity that is requested by the interruption. Writing it down removes it from your mind, and it also assures you that it will be thought of in future planning. If you're sure you won't handle the new activity today, then you can write it directly on the Activity Inventory sheet and add a deadline and a *U* for unplanned. Or you can write it on the bottom of your To Do Today sheet, under the header Unplanned & Urgent.

Then write a dash (minus) to the right of the activity that you're currently working on.

Finally, intensify your determination to finish the Pomodoro that you started before the interruption.

4.15 Void

One time, no less than eight people suddenly showed up at my desk. Apparently every single member of my team needed me for something:

Team: *Did you recently check in some new code to the archive?*

Staffan: *It depends on how you define "recently."*

Team: *Less than five minutes ago.*

Staffan: *Eh, yes, I guess so. Is something wrong?*

Team: *Right now, none of us can do anything. The code you checked in doesn't compile!*

This is not the time and place to inform them that I'm in the middle of a Pomodoro and that they are welcome to come back another day. Clearly it's better to void my Pomodoro than to not respond to their urgent and reasonable request. After helping them, I take a short break and then wind up the clock for 25 minutes and start to focus again.

4.16 External Interruptions Strategy

To summarize, you need to be aware of the type and amount of external interruptions. You do that by tracking every interruption with a dash and writing down the title of the requested activity.

The strategy for handling external interruptions is a four-stage one:

1. *Inform*: "I'm in the middle of something."

2. *Negotiate*: "Is it OK if I come back to you on Friday?"

3. *Schedule*: Write down the title of the activity and later plan it for a future Pomodoro.

4. *Call back*: Call back as you have promised; otherwise, you will not be entrusted with this responsibility anymore.

4.17 Interruption Notation

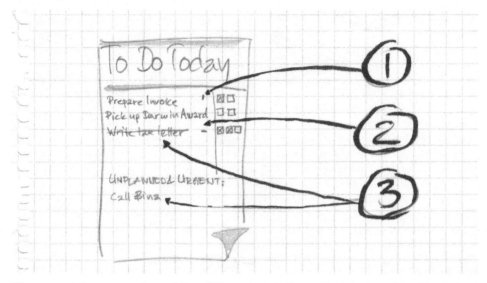

Here are a few examples of the different notations that I use when I'm interrupted. Say I'm starting this day by selecting three activities: "Prepare invoice," "Pick up Darwin Award," and "Write tax letter." It's always important to correspond with the tax authority, so I take that activity first. After the first Pomodoro, I mark the first box with an X. After two Pomodori, I have completed my tax letter and continue by preparing my invoice. I put an X in the second box because I have completed a Pomodoro, and I cross out the tax letter item on the To Do Today sheet because it is complete. So, what are the 1, 2, and 3 in the picture here?

1. While preparing the invoice, I got an internal interruption: out of nowhere, I remembered that I must call Edda. I wrote it down on the Activity Inventory sheet to do it another day. Then I put an apostrophe next to the title for preparing invoices. This is tracking that will be summarized at the end of the day.

2. Bina called me while I was writing the tax letter. I told her that I'm in the middle of something and asked if I could call her later. This was an external interruption, so I added a dash next to the tax letter title. Once again, this is tracking that will be summarized at the end of the day.

3. After writing the dash, I also wrote "Call Bina" under Unplanned & Urgent.

4.18 Aware of the Extent

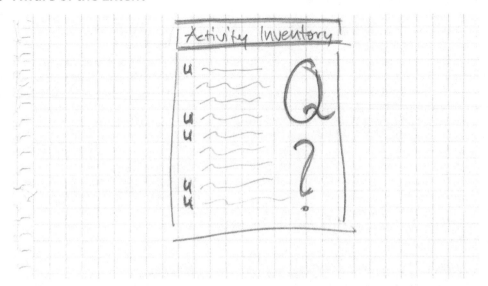

What's the number of *U* marked activities on my Activity Inventory sheet, and how many Unplanned & Urgent activities do I have on my To Do Today sheet? By looking at these metrics, I can assess my planning capability.

If I have many unplanned activities, it implies that I miss a lot when I plan in the morning. It's a qualitative error. I didn't expect all these things to be included. The next morning I can check more carefully to see whether I have included everything in my commitment.

You're always allowed to reassess priorities between each Pomodoro, and there's nothing wrong with doing that. But if you always select some activities in the morning and always realize at the end of the day that the majority of activities actually completed during this day were outside this initial selection, then you will not feel the sense of commitment when you plan. If you don't feel committed, then you won't feel rewarded when you summarize your day. Chiefly, there will be no difference between the Activity Inventory and To Do Today sheets. Both will include a bunch of activities that you "might" do today.

4.19 Self-Reflection on Interruptions

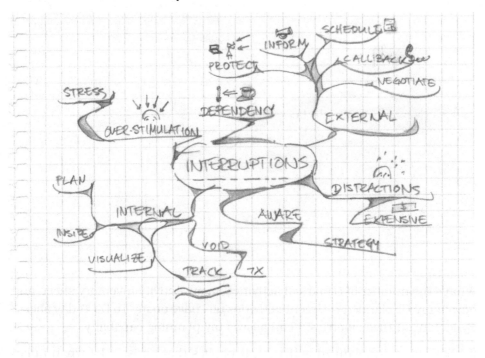

- What type of interruptions do you get at work?

- How do you act when someone bothers you with an irrelevant question?

- How do you store the new good ideas that suddenly pop up?

- When do you have difficulty concentrating on only one activity?

- Do you always come back later when you have promised to do that?

CHAPTER 5

Estimate

5.1 A Cucumber and an Artichoke Meet at the Races

Artichoke: Number five will win.

Cucumber: How do you know?

Artichoke: He won when I was here last week.

Cucumber: Today's race was run last week?

Artichoke: Of course not. Each race is unique.

Cucumber: So, he might not win today. He may get injured in the middle of the race or just have a bad day. The horses he is running against today may be faster.

Artichoke: Sure.

Cucumber: So, you can't guarantee that number five will win.

Artichoke: No, it's a guess. But based on what I know right now, it's my best guess.

Cucumber: But it's not a sure thing?

Artichoke: No, just a guess based on empirical knowledge.

5.2   Measurements and Guesses

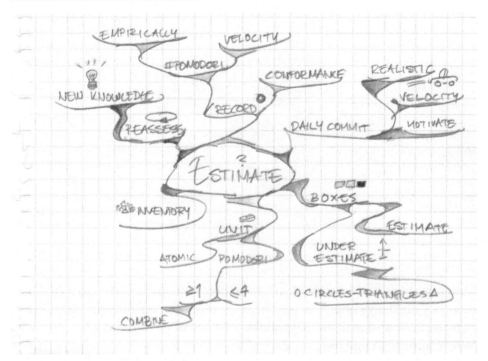

Estimating future achievements is basically guessing. So, why not use the history and assume it will repeat itself?

Estimation and measurement are two essential parts of the Pomodoro Technique. Without them, it is very difficult to make a daily plan. As you work on the technique, you will only improve if you take the time to look back. Then you'll see how what you thought you could do maps to what you actually achieved. Tracking and recording are the Pomodoro Technique ways of measurement. In this chapter, you'll learn how to estimate.

5.3 Estimates on Your Activity Inventory Sheet

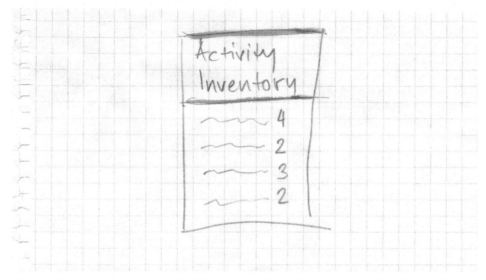

Commitment is a vital part of the Pomodoro Technique. The To Do Today sheet is your daily commitment. The collection of items on your sheet must be reasonable and realistic. The quantity of activities is about what you normally complete in one day.

If there is a recurring discrepancy between your estimates and the actual effort you have spent on an activity, then there can be two types of error sources:

- Your estimate process or your estimate ability is not good enough.

- New information appeared after you started this activity, and it changed the circumstances.

You can't predict what new information or changing circumstances will show up. But you can empirically improve your skills in estimating with training and monitoring. Every morning, before you plan the day, try looking at each new activity on your Activity Inventory sheet and estimating the number of Pomodori it will take to complete it. You can also quickly glance at your existing estimates and see whether any need to be revised.

For example, I write my estimates to the right of the activity items on the Activity Inventory sheet. Of course, I use a pencil so that I can change the numbers if I later gain knowledge that makes me want to modify my estimate.

5.4 Wisdom of Crowds

James Surowiecki writes about a crowd at a county fair that almost perfectly guessed the weight of an ox—on average. No one was as close to the right answer as the average of all guesses was. Why? If the crowd consists of partly experts in this subject matter, then each one will add some knowledge, and their errors will sum up to zero.[1]

Psychologist Edward Vul showed in an experiment that averaging multiple guesses from one person about a fact provides a better estimate than any single guess. He asked people various trivia questions. Without telling them, he repeated some of the questions a moment later. He noticed then that the average of a person's answers was more correct than any of the person's single guesses. Why? Cognition is based on statistical inference. For example, trying to answer a trivia question creates a range of possible values in my head. Every time I answer, I unconsciously just pick one of these values. The average of my answers is close to perfect, but their standard deviation is far from zero.[2]

So, crowds know more than any single person making a single guess, and you can become your own crowd by reassessing the situation. From time to time you make a new guess even though no new information has emerged.

_____

1. *The Wisdom of Crowds [Sur05]*
2. *Go ahead, change your mind [Bra08]*

5.5 Activity Size

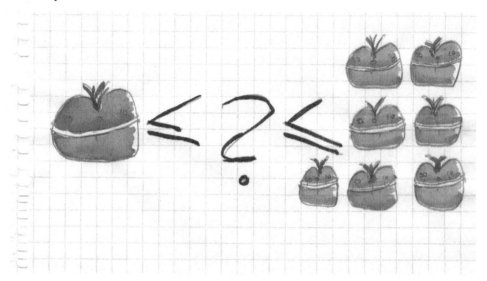

The currency that is used for estimation is the Pomodoro. You must decide how many Pomodori you need to spend on an activity. An estimate of four means that you predict that you will spend four Pomodori on this activity before it's done. Since a Pomodoro is atomic, you can't use numbers like 1/2 or 2.2 Pomodori.

When you estimate that an activity will take more than seven Pomodori, then it's too complex. You'll need to break down the activity. Each subactivity will have a separate line on the Activity Inventory sheet and a separate estimate. There is no precision in gigantic estimates.

When you estimate that an activity will take less than one Pomodoro, then you can indicate that by putting a zero next to this activity. This does not tell you that it will take zero Pomodoro to complete, just that it takes less than one. These activities should occupy one row each on the Activity Inventory sheet.

You can then combine a few of these less-than-one-Pomodoro activities when you select the activities for my To Do Today sheet. Put them on the same line, demonstrating that they are one unit today.

5.6 Choose

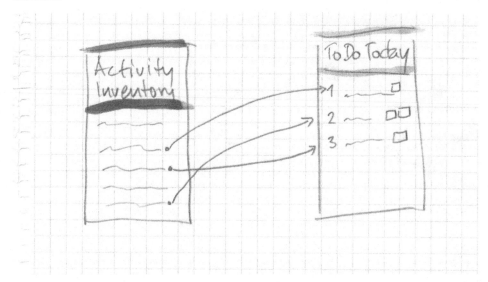

Planning based on estimates makes your commitment for the day more realistic, and as a result, your motivation will improve. Recording the number of completed Pomodoro every day gives you a good understanding of your Pomodoro velocity.

When you select the most important activities from the Activity Inventory sheet in the morning, their estimated sum should not be higher than your empirically established velocity. You then write the activities on your To Do Today sheet and add as many small boxes to each line as you've estimated this activity to take.

Every time the clock rings and you have finished a Pomodoro, write an X next to the current activity. This means that you have done 25 minutes of effort on this activity.

Then three things can happen. You can run out of boxes before you have completed the whole activity. In that case, you underestimated this activity. Or, you can complete the whole activity before you run out of boxes, or you can complete it exactly on schedule. In the latter two cases, you cross out the activity on your To Do Today sheet.

5.7 Quantitative Estimate Error

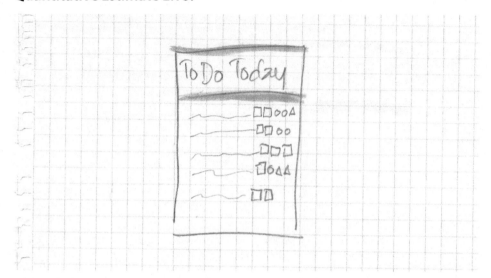

What if you run out of boxes before you have completed the whole activity? You have estimated this activity to last for a number of Pomodori, and now you have used them all and still the activity is not done.

Then you reestimate. You guess how many more Pomodori you will need to complete this activity. Then you write as many circles next to the boxes as you estimate your remaining Pomodori to be. Now you can continue to write an X in the circles every time the clock rings and you have finished a 25-minute Pomodoro.

If you run out of circles as well, then you can make a third and final reestimate. This time, write the same amount of triangles, next to the circles, as the new delta.

To not complete the activity, even in the limit of the third reestimate, is a failure. You need to analyze why you under-estimate again and again. Maybe your activities should be smaller and less complex. Estimating complex activities has low precision by nature.

5.8   Yesterday's Weather

As you know by now, one Pomodoro is a 25-minute iteration. Multiple Pomodori are surrounded by a larger daily iteration. Each day starts with planning and ends with the retrospective. In a Pomodoro, you should allow yourself to focus on only one activity. But how many activities should you plan for one day?

A national weather service spent a gigantic amount of money on a new forecast system. All the emerging technology was included, and it had an accuracy rate of almost 70 percent. Then a clever person challenged the super machine with a much simpler algorithm. It was called Yesterday's Weather, and it said, "Tomorrow will be like today." Guess what? It had the same accuracy as the super machine.

Estimating future achievements is basically guessing. So, why not use the history and assume it will repeat itself? If you can quantify your achievements every day, then this is presumably your velocity tomorrow as well. By measuring the number of Pomodoro every day, you can even fine-tune your velocity continuously with an average.[3]

---

3.   *Extreme Programming Explained: Embrace Change [Bec00]*

5.9   Estimates on Records Sheet

At the end of the day, make sure to record your tracking data on the Records sheet. You can then add two columns for each estimate.

Here's the process: first, I write down the number of remaining boxes for each activity that I have completed today. Suppose that I over-estimated one activity by three Pomodori (+3), I over-estimated two activities by two Pomodori each (+2 and +2), and I under-estimated one activity by two Pomodori (-2). All in all I have added five boxes too many on the To Do Today sheet. My total estimate error is +5.

Second, I use the rightmost column for the number of reestimates. How many rows have circles (one reestimate) or circles and triangles (two reestimates)?

The goal is to get zeroes in both these columns. But since one source of estimate errors is the changing world and new problem knowledge, there will always be discrepancies between estimates and actually used Pomodori. Anyway, the sum of the first column should be zero. New problem knowledge both reduces and increases activity density. In the long run, these errors should cancel each other out.

5.10 Drum-Buffer-Rope

The average number of Pomodori that you complete per day is your *drum rhythm*. The sum of all the estimates that you have on your Activity Inventory sheet is your *buffer*. The *rope* is how the constraint signals to the upstream process when to slow down or speed up the pace.

The rope starts in your hand and ends in the buffer. With it, you can pull new activities to your workbench. When the buffer is filled, the rope becomes slacker. When the buffer is empty, the rope is stretched to its maximum. You pull, but there are no new activities.

You need to avoid both feast and famine syndromes. The feast syndrome occurs when you have too many activities on your Activity Inventory sheet. Some activities may stay there a long time with no progress. An Activity Inventory sheet like this is inflexible, discouraging, and even misleading. The famine syndrome is the opposite—a short Activity Inventory sheet might on a creative day turn up to be empty. The theory of constraints teaches you how to trim the size of your Activity Inventory so that you can avoid both the feast and famine syndromes.

If I complete nine Pomodori per day and I want to have ten days of buffer, then the sum of all my estimates in my Activity Inventory sheet should be approximately 90. If 90 is significantly exceeded, I must prioritize. If it drops far below 90, I can add more to the inventory. If I have a boss or a client filling up much of my Activity Inventory sheet, then I may need to ask for their help in prioritizing or adding to my list.[4]

5.11 Self-Reflection on Estimate

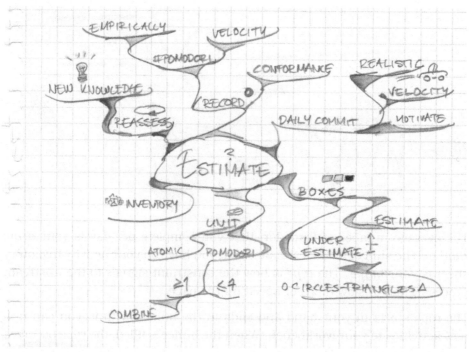

- Do you normally keep up with what you have planned for your workday?

- Do you ever change an estimate afterward?

- Do you know how long it would take to do all the things that you have promised?

- How big can your activity estimate be—in days, hours, minutes?

- How small can your activity estimate be—in days, hours, minutes?

---

4. *The Goal [Gol04]*

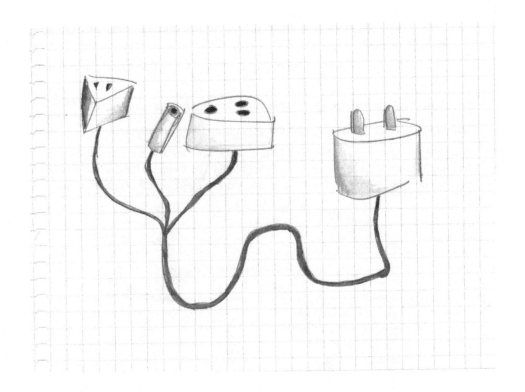

CHAPTER 6

Adapt

6.1   A Cucumber and an Artichoke Meet at the Movie Theater

Cucumber: *Hey Art! What's up, man?*

Artichoke: *Now that I've been doing the Pomodoro thing for a week, I've invented a derivate that I call PomdoroButt.[1]*

Cucumber: *Pomo...what?*

Artichoke: *Well, I'm doing The Pomodoro Technique right out of the box...*

- *...But, my iterations are two hours. I really want to progress.*

- *...But, I have no problem with activities lasting for weeks as long as I feel that they are important. Breaking them down just gets me more things to keep in mind.*

- *...But, I don't use a kitchen timer. If I use timeboxing, I always have to stop while in the flow.*

- *...But, I don't retrospect at the end of the day. I know I've found the optimum process now.*

Cucumber: *Have you heard of the Dreyfus model of skills acquisition?*

Artichoke: *Do you mean Richard Dreyfuss from the Jaws movie?*

Cucumber: *Never mind. However, I think you should stick to the original Pomodoro Technique—exactly as it is designed—for at least two weeks. Then, when you have really experienced pros and cons, you can start to make small adjustments.*

---

1.   The ScrumButt Test, aka the Nokia Test, for Scrum teams was originally developed at Nokia Siemens Networks.

6.2 Tweaking

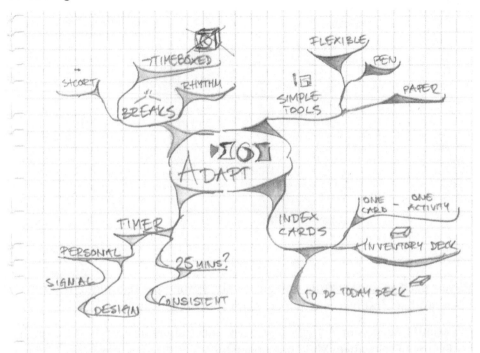

To avoid interrupting my other activities every time I receive an email, I can set aside two Pomodori a day for responding.

When you know how to implement Pomodoro Technique the usual way, you may feel tempted to tweak it. That's good. That's why you collect and track data, and that's why you have your daily retrospectives. But don't tweak anything until you've tried the usual way for at least two weeks. You need experience in order to know what is good and bad for you. In this chapter, I share tweaks that I have done.

6.3   Simple Tools

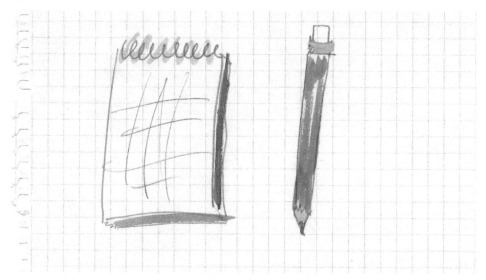

All you need to successfully implement the Pomodoro Technique is a timer, a pen, and several pieces of paper. Keep your tools simple.

You should keep your Activity Inventory sheet short and up-to-date to give it a feeling of relevance. Mine has space for 25 to 30 activities.

But, after a few weeks, my Activity Inventory sheet is a muddle. When there's no room left, I review every item that has not been completed. If the activity is not completed but still pertinent, then I copy the item to a fresh Activity Inventory sheet. After that, I can discard the old sheet.

You might be tempted to use software to keep track of your activities. You can, but the simple tools are the best. With simple tools, you change the rules for your notation without delay and without involving a software maintenance team. The usual advantages of software, such as long-term storage, bulk distribution, heavy processing, or allowing for many simultaneous users, are not relevant to the Activity Inventory sheet.

6.4   Index Cards

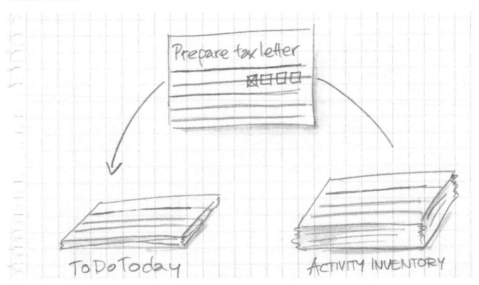

The Activity Inventory sheet and the To Do Today sheet do not have to be two sheets of paper. One alternative is to keep each single activity on its own index card.

I take a fresh card every time I realize that I must add a new activity to the Activity Inventory sheet. Then I write the title of the activity at the top of the card with a black felt-tip pen. Below the title I can add diagrams, phone numbers, web addresses, or anything else relevant to complete this activity. This kind of nice-to-have scribble should not be as conspicuous as the title, so I use a pencil for extra information. Finally, I add the same number of boxes as I estimate that it will take—in Pomodoro time—to finish the activity.

Therefore, my Activity Inventory sheet is now a deck of index cards. Each card describes one activity. I select an amount of cards every morning during the Planning stage. This selection is my daily commitment: my To Do Today deck. It's ordered with the most important activity card on top. You can try this approach or find one that works for you.

6.5 Administrative Pomodoro

The best way to start with the Pomodoro Technique is with a pure, simple approach. After a while, you might want to optimize the process for your personal circumstances. For example, I might usually spend a significant part of the day writing emails. To avoid interrupting my other activities every time I receive an email, I can set aside two Pomodori a day for responding. Here are some examples:

- *Advanced adaption example #1*: I always use my first Pomodoro in the morning for sending responses to emails received since I went home yesterday. And if 25 minutes isn't enough, I don't continue writing until lunch, destroying my whole schedule. Instead, since I know that I will have another dedicated email-writing Pomodoro every day immediately after lunch, I stop writing emails after 25 minutes.

- *Advanced adaption example #2*: I usually drop in at the office about 45 minutes before the morning meeting. That's when I can customize a 40-minute Pomodoro for things I need to do every morning. Keeping a checklist for these morning activities guarantees that I won't just hang around without any goal. Unfortunately, this 40-minute Pomodoro is not comparable to Pomodori of other sizes. If all the other Pomodori last for 25 minutes, then I'm not counting the 40-minute administrative Pomodoro in the Record stage.

6.6 Sound and Shape

When I started to practice the Pomodoro Technique, I was convinced that the clock ticking would disturb me. So, I put the clock on a piece of cloth to reduce the resonance. After practicing the Pomodoro Technique for a few months, I couldn't concentrate without the ticking. I had trained a reflex that enabled me to focus.

One clock must not control more than one person, pair, or chat group. Do not synchronize the Pomodori in a diversified group. What happens otherwise if only one person wants to void his Pomodoro?

Various clock properties suit different office environments. I have found that I benefit from sounds, gestures, and visibility. For example, winding up the clock gives me a clear signal and a visible front for my rhythm and conditioned reflexes. It's also an advantage to me if my clock counts down, since the time left is much more interesting than the time that is gone. The environment decides whether a mechanical kitchen timer, a digital timer, an hourglass, a mobile phone, or computer software is most proper. But when you keep your clock visible on the desk, your teammates become aware of your technique and subconsciously more inclined to respect it. Try to find a personal design. Unfortunately, the shape of a tomato doesn't give any advantage, but red is a color that most people can't ignore!

6.7 Length of Pomodori

Is the number 25 magic? Is there any research that says that a 25-minute focused session is the optimum? Not as far as I know. I'm even pretty sure that it's impossible to find a worldwide optimum session time. It depends on who you are. It depends on your type of activities. It depends on who you work with and what responsibilities you have to them. It depends on if you're tired, or if you're in good spirits on a particular day.

Short iterations are more often completed. If you are constantly interrupted, it indicates that you should shorten your Pomodoro length. It's easier to stay focused all the way through when you have smaller iterations. If the iterations are longer, there are fewer breaks, but on the other hand, the breaks tend to be longer as well.

Every Pomodoro Technique practitioner has the option to experiment and find her own optimum. But I urge you to start with 25 minutes and stick to the same length for at least two weeks. Changing the length all the time destroys your rhythm.

6.8   Length of Breaks

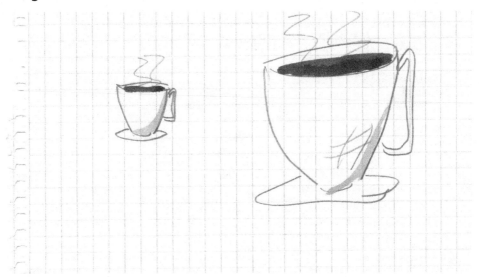

The default schedule in the Pomodoro Technique—three small breaks followed by one longer break—is not mandatory. It depends on what you do and who you are, including where you work and how you feel. Complex problems may demand longer breaks. If you're tired one day, that can also be a reason to lengthen the breaks.

However, if breaks are too long, then you will lose the rhythm. Every Pomodoro start will feel like starting on a new activity. If you skip breaks, on the other hand, then quality will fall. You will get an attention deficit that you must pay for later the same day. Furthermore, if you randomly mix long and short breaks, you will not feel motivated to wind up the clock. The setup time will increase, since it's all about biological rhythms.

Should the breaks be timeboxed? Will this stop drifting? No, because you need to be mentally ready when you start your next Pomodoro. There is no point in jumping into an activity if you're still daydreaming. A new Pomodoro Technique practitioner who has problems coming back after breaks might timebox them for a week. In the longer run, you should rely on rhythm.

6.9 Progress Sheet

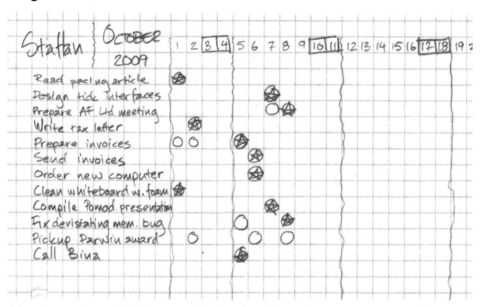

When I see the same activity title recurrently show up on my To Do Today sheet without being done, then I do a variant of the Activity Inventory sheet, which I call the Progress sheet.

I take an A4 sheet with 5x5 mm squares and type the name of the month and my name in the upper-left corner. Then I write, along the short side of the paper, this month's days from right to left (31, 30, 29, and so on, down to 1), with one number in each box. That gives me about a 5 cm margin on the left side. I write all the known activities in that margin, one activity per line. My Progress sheet then replaces the Activity Inventory sheet forever. You can see the progress sheet as an alternative implementation of the concept Activity Inventory. What's the Records sheet for then? The Records sheet is for tracking whatever I'm tracking, such as the number of phone calls.

Every morning when I select activities for my To Do Today sheet, I'll also draw a circle in the square where the column with today's date meets the row with the activity that I have chosen. At the end of the day when I do my daily retrospective, I draw a star in every ring where the activity was completed. If I have many empty circles, it means that I often overestimate my daily commitment. And activities with many starless circles probably need to be broken down.

6.10 Priority Tournament

When I'm not sure what activities to choose for my To Do Today sheet, then I do a priority tournament. First, I write down the titles of all the activities that are candidates—one activity title per scrap of paper. I then put all the scraps in an unprioritized pile. After that, I take the top two and compare. Which one would I rather have done today if I can do only one? Whichever loses goes to the loser pile to the left of the unprioritized pile, and the winner stays in my hand.

Then I take the next scrap from the unprioritized pile and compare it with the winner from the first game. I will continue like that, game after game. The winner remains in my hand, and the loser goes to the loser pile. I have a winner of the whole tournament when the unprioritized pile is empty. The highest prioritized activity is in my hand.

But I can complete more than one activity per day. Therefore, I make a new tournament with the loser pile. Actually, I do as many tournaments as the number of activities that I estimate that I can complete today. I write all the winners on my To Do Today sheet until the amount is a realistic commitment for today.

This process may sound trivial, but it is a lot easier to compare the priority of just two activities than to extract a prioritized group from a long list. I often get a different result than if I just look at the Activity Inventory sheet and choose activities freely. Again, this is because of our limited working memory.[2]

---

2. *Manage Your Project Portfolio: Increase Your Capacity and Finish More Projects [Rot09]*

6.11 Inbox to Zero

I never accidentally glance through my email inbox in the middle of a Pomodoro dedicated to some other activity. When, however, I have planned to read and act on my emails, then I apply the "Inbox to Zero" principle. David Allen describes it as a three-step process:[3]

1. Start from the top.
2. Take one thing at a time.
3. Never put something back into the inbox.

I think about the next action for every new email. If it takes a minute or less to answer, then I'll do it immediately. If I can delegate it further, then I delegate it right now. When I know it's an activity that I will do but that takes a little longer, then I don't start it now. I write the item on my Activity Inventory sheet, move the email to an archive folder, and mentally drop the activity.

Activities that I can't do because I need information from other people are similar to the delegated activities. I'll send the request to that person and then move the email to an archive folder.

I also always think about whether I will benefit from this email in the future; otherwise, I delete it immediately. Loads of emails that will never lead to any action creates information overflow. It hides the emails that are new, that are important, and that really require action.

---

3. *Getting Things Done: The Art of Stress-Free Productivity* [All02]

6.12 Repeated Reviews

Your memory capacity can be improved. According to Tony Buzan, "A general guideline here is to review shortly after the learning period or daily event has occurred, to review one day later, to review a third time one week later, to review a fourth time one month later, and to review a fifth time three to six months later."

Every time you think of something, the resistance to connecting these memories in your brain decreases. It's like clearing a path through a forest. The more times you walk this path, the fewer impediments there will be.

Thoughts become famous inside your head. And just like pop stars, publicity increases the chances of getting more publicity. By repeating an important conclusion, you can increase the probability that you will recall it at a proper time.[4]

_____

4.   *The Mind Map Book [BB96]*

6.13 Daily Mind Map

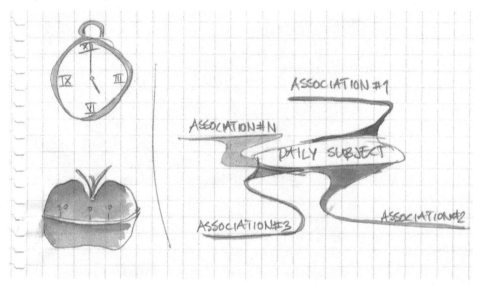

While using the Pomodoro Technique, you need to reserve some time at the end of the day for review. You don't need to spend an entire Pomodoro on reviewing what you have done that day and on preparing for the next day. When you have one Pomodoro's worth or less, you can wind up your kitchen timer for whatever time is left, such as 10 minutes. Use the back side of the To Do Today sheet, and rotate it 90 degrees so it is in landscape orientation. Now you're ready to explore your mind in order to grasp at the most usable knowledge concluded today.

This is how I do the next step: in the middle of the paper, I draw a picture of my daily subject. What's my daily subject? What have I been communicating most with colleagues today? What's the keyword of the activity with most Xs drawn today? What was the subject of the meetings I went to today? What tool did I use in a new way today? Those are a lot of questions with possibly many answers. I have to choose one single thing as my daily subject. I pick the first one that pops up in mind and that feels outstanding in some aspect.

Then I draw an ordinary mind map with colored branches, small icons, and free associations. When the timer rings, I just put the To Do Today sheet with my daily mind map into my pile of past daily mind maps. Once a month I will end the work day with a review of the previous month's pile of mind maps to repeat what I've learned.

6.14 Prescriptive and Adaptive

There are many time management processes, and to some extent they recommend the same techniques, tools, and philosophies.[5] They help us optimize how we spend our time—or more correctly, how we spend our attention—by planning, goal setting, monitoring, recapping, and prioritizing. The Pomodoro Technique may not add entirely new tools or ideas. So, what distinguishes Pomodoro Technique then?

The Pomodoro Technique is prescriptive. Having simple and concrete best practices makes it easy to get started. It could mean that it does not suit all people or contexts. But the Pomodoro Technique has adaptiveness built in.

The Pomodoro Technique gets us to focus on execution. It could mean that we ignore *Systems Thinking [Sen94]* and holism. That's why it's often beneficial to let processes like *Scrum [Sch04], XP [Bec00],* or GTD enclose the Pomodoro Technique.

The Pomodoro Technique has a few simple artifacts. Three blank sheets and a kitchen timer is all that you need to get started. The simplicity also gives you flexibility. Adjusting a computer-based tool can be unattainable.

---

5. *Get Everything Done [For00], Zen To Done [Bab08], Getting Things Done [All02], The Now Habit [Fio07],* and *The 7 Habits of Highly Effective People [Cov94]* are a few examples.

6.15 Ring Disquiet

Is the Pomodoro Technique suitable for everybody? Maybe not. But I recommend you try it before you say "no thanks." There are some types of people who I think would be better off with Pomodoro Technique than they might first think.

For instance, a person who wants to be inspired before he starts anything might refuse to use the Pomodoro Technique. Nonetheless, he's the person who needs a process like this most. In the morning selection, he gains a commitment instead of all these messy threads circling around in his head. Furthermore, when he allocates priority in his To Do Today sheet and chooses just one activity there—the most significant one—his arousal will be amplified even more. And if that is not enough, the clock-winding gesture will light his fire. These are the mechanics to get the inspiration that he was waiting for.

A person who wants to turbo-drive when he's in the zone might also turn down the Pomodoro Technique. But he would be helped by this kind of process, too. Concentrating fully on an activity is not equivalent to being fully productive. He will easily be bogged down in trivia. He spends hour after hour with some problem that seems extremely important to him. Taking a step back every half hour will show him the big picture. And small regular breaks will give him the sustainable pace as a replacement for struggling with increasing amounts of internal distractions.

6.16 Self-Reflection on Adapt

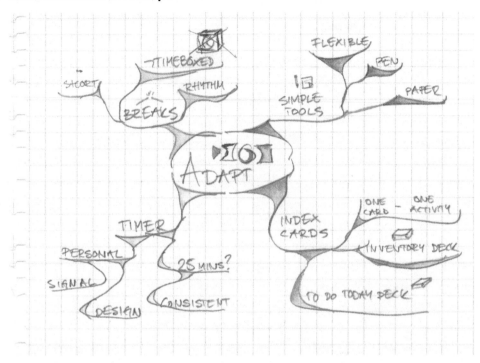

- For what type of administrative activities do you use a pen and paper?

- At what time of the workday do you make phone calls or send emails?

- How long is your normal break?

- When do you concentrate for too long without taking a break?

- How do you use index cards in your work?

CHAPTER 7

Team

7.1 A Cucumber and an Artichoke Meet in the Conference Room

Artichoke: *I tried the Pomodoro Technique yesterday at a meeting.*

Cucumber: *What happened?*

Artichoke: *I wound up my kitchen timer to 25 minutes, put the clock in front of me, and then just closed my eyes.*

Cucumber: *What happened when someone asked you a question?*

Artichoke: *I just said, "I can't answer now; can't you see I'm in the middle of a Pomodoro?"*

Cucumber: *How did it go?*

Artichoke: *I don't know. When the clock rang, I stepped up to the whiteboard, drew a mammoth X, and then left the room.*

Cucumber: *You didn't really do that, did you?*

Artichoke: *No. Honestly, I couldn't see how to apply the technique, so we just had an ordinary meeting.*

Cucumber: *Meetings can be ideal for 25-minute, kitchen-timer-controlled, time-boxed iterations.*

Artichoke: *But what about those situations where the Pomodoro Technique doesn't apply?*

Cucumber: *They are less frequent than you might expect. But when you can't apply the Pomodoro Technique, it's still possible to track those activities if you want.*

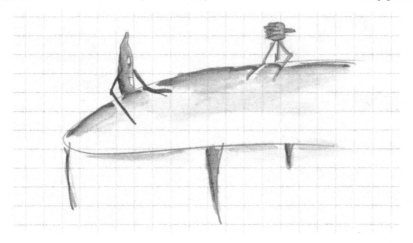

7.2 Working with Others

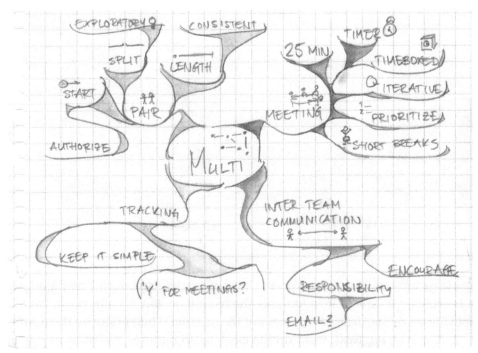

To promote communication within the team, you can decide to not count team-member-to-team-member questions as external interruptions.

So far in this book we've looked at the Pomodoro Technique as a personal time management process. But since it's adaptive by nature, it's not limited to isolated individuals. In this chapter, you will see that Pomodoro Technique can also be used in a collaborative environment—for example, in pair work, in meetings, and in teams.

7.3 Timeboxed Meetings

Meetings are one of the most perfect places for the Pomodoro Technique. In this section I'll explain how to apply the technique. On a whiteboard, list all activities or all the desired outcomes of the meeting. Then prioritize them with 1, 2, 3, and so on. Next, wind up the clock to 25 minutes and start focusing —as a group—on the first-priority activity.

When the clock rings, stop immediately. As you know, you always have short breaks between Pomodori. Perhaps someone wants to visit the restroom. Then, after the break, you can decide which activity to go on with before you wind up the clock again.

A meeting without breaks turns into a yawn-fest within one hour. On many occasions, it's a slumber long before that.

If you finish the meeting halfway through a Pomodoro, then you should try to over-learn as a group. You can review what you have done, try to improve it, or make inferences—until the clock rings.

Note that your meeting pals don't have to be firm believers in the Pomodoro Technique. They just need to obey the kitchen timer if they want a productive meeting.

7.4 Tracking Meetings

What if your suggestion for using the Pomodoro Technique for meetings in your company is falling on deaf ears? And if a meeting doesn't turn out as well as it could have, do you still write an X on your To Do Today sheet?

The answer is that it depends on how you define your X. Writing an X every time the clock rings is one way of implementing the Tracking stage. It's good to track easily measured metrics that don't have complicated meanings. If your Xs mean "25-minute effort units spent working alone at your desk," for example, then you don't write an X after a meeting.

You choose your own metrics. It is not mandatory to track any particular metric, and no metric is universally prohibited. I keep the number of metrics down to avoid being overwhelmed by administrative work. Every type of metric I choose is there simply because I believe today that it may show me how to improve my process for tomorrow. If I suspect that meetings are not giving back the value they cost me, then I could write a Y for meetings and an X for ordinary Pomodori.

7.5   Pair Work Rhythm

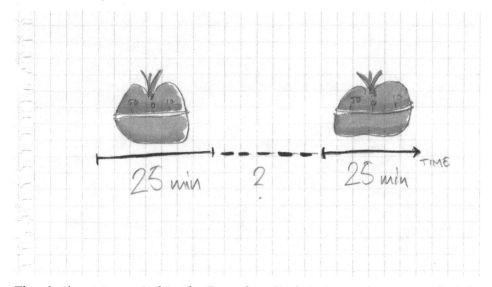

The rhythm is essential in the Pomodoro Technique, and it's controlled by the length of the breaks. Participants need to be mentally ready at the start of a new Pomodoro. When doing the Pomodoro Technique individually, this is easy. I won't wind up the timer until I am in the right mood. In a pair Pomodoro, you need to be more cautious. Both of the people must be in a state of preparedness. And it's not a matter of sitting and waiting for that to happen. You can influence your readiness. The break starts when the clock rings, that is, as a signal of the previous Pomodoro ending. At that time, we tell each other the following:

- What we will do during the break

- Our estimate of how long it will take

We don't need to be detailed about the first item, and no one will punish us if the estimate isn't exactly correct. My collaboration partner might say, "I need to make a phone call; it'll take about five minutes." This will make us aware of the size of the break already from the beginning.

7.6 Authorizing Pomodoro Start

When working in pairs, how can the person winding up the clock be sure that his partner has mentally finished what he did during the last break? The answer is quite easy. Both your pairing partner and you should authorize your commitment to start a new Pomodoro. If the authorization isn't complete, the transition of state—from break to work—is not legitimate. This is analogous to authorizing a bank customer before his money can be transmitted to another account.

The authorization can be more or less formal. One way is to ask out loud, "Are you ready?" Then wait for the mandatory positive response from the partner. Another way is to move a personal token. Each team member pets her own personal soft toy animal. I'm fond of soft toy bloodhounds. Before winding up the clock to start a Pomodoro, both my pairing partner and I need to put our pets on the desk in a free area. When the clock rings as a signal for break, the pets are removed from this free area. Does exposing your favorite soft toy animal make you feel silly? Well, use your mobile phone as a token. This is conditioned reflexes in practice!

7.7   Pair Pomodoro Length

Are the Pomodoro iterations lengthened or shortened when working in pairs? Neither. First, try 25 minutes for at least a week. If it feels too short or too long, then try another length for at least a week.

Short Pomodori create more process ceremony compared to doing real work. Long Pomodori make it harder to focus all the time and harder to cut the day into small releases. Your interpair communication can be a heavy effort in a long Pomodoro. On the other hand, pair chatting takes some time, and it's still important that each Pomodoro increases your accumulated work result.

Again, you don't want to change the length too often, since then you can't use the number of completed Pomodori as an effort metric. Suppose that you have 25-minute Pomodori on Monday, a 40-minute Pomodoro on Tuesday, and a 20-minute Pomodoro on Wednesday. How should you compare each day's efforts? The number 25 is not a holy grail, but try it at least for two weeks. If you're not satisfied, then try another length for at least another week.

7.8   Split a Pair Temporarily

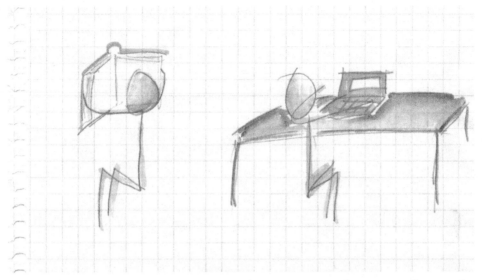

Sometimes you come to a point where the emerging task is more of a search-and-investigate nature, not a normal constructive collaboration task. Then it could be easier to split up for a Pomodoro. "I look for this, you look for that, and then we meet again after the next Pomodoro break." Still, when you work independently, you need to be in sync if your ambition is to resume pairing later.

Say my work partner needs to take a longer break from our shared work task. Maybe he's scheduled for a meeting for the next 35 minutes. When he tells me this, I ask him whether I can go on solo with our joint work task for one Pomodoro. If the nature of this task does not allow a single person to go on, then I have to come up with some other tasks for myself until my partner comes back.

Sometimes it can be more fruitful to split apart for one Pomodoro just to get two independent views on a problem. We go apart and do two parallel and individual brainstorms. When the clock rings and after a small break, we join up and explain our new results to each other.

7.9 Tracking Pair Work

There are many seldom stated truths about process metrics:

- You need a big sample in order to draw any conclusions from metrics.

- Apples shouldn't be compared to pears.

- Metrics hardly ever show up with a good-to-bad scale.

If you change collaboration partners every morning, then it's hard to compare the five Pomodori when you worked with Lisa on Monday with the seven Pomodori when you worked with Fred on Tuesday. Lisa might have key knowledge for this project and needs to spend some time helping other teammates. The most valuable metrics are those collected while you work with a recurring partner.

But you don't want to be caught up in details. Even though measuring with different partners is not perfect, it will give you feedback. Frequently changing partner is a fluctuating source of error for your tracking. In the long run, it should even itself out, however.

7.10 Team Culture

Every team has to find its own culture. By culture, I mean "the way we do things here." To promote communication within the team, you can decide to not count team-member-to-team-member questions as external interruptions. It's like tolerating two activities in every Pomodoro:

- The chosen activity from the To Do Today sheet

- Work-related, interteam communication

This agreement entails an additional responsibility. Before you start to communicate with a teammate who's obeying his ticking clock, you need to consider whether you need the answer immediately. Otherwise, you might use an asynchronous communication channel, such as sending an email or passing a brief slip of paper.

7.11 Self-Reflection on Team

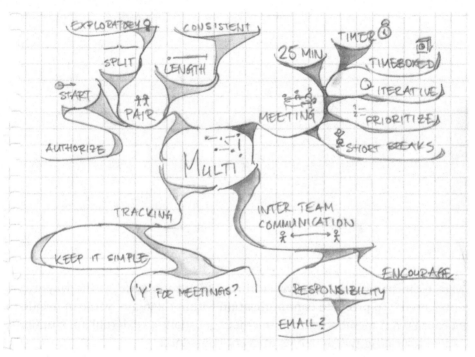

- How long are your meetings?

- After how much time do you take a break when you work in pairs?

- After how much time do you take a break when you work in groups?

- What type of activities are not suitable for pair work?

- Do you start your meetings even if everyone isn't ready?

Process Map

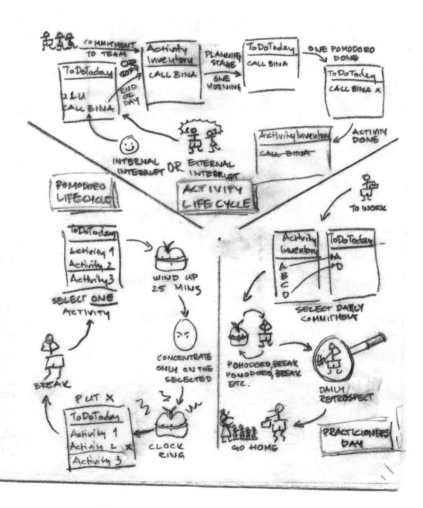

Resources

Pomodoro timer

Search for pomodoro+timer+download.

Personally, I prefer a robust mechanical kitchen timer. If you opt for software, you will find it on the Internet for most operating systems, phone models, and virtual machines.

Discussion groups

Search for Pomodoro Technique at http://groups.google.com

There are two groups on Google Groups. One focuses on desktop timers, while the other one has general discussions about the Pomodoro Technique.

The official Pomodoro Techniques site

http://www.pomodorotechnique.com

Francesco Cirillo invented the Pomodoro Technique, and he also maintains the official site. There you can find the official book, written by Francesco. He also shares templates for To Do Today sheet and Activity Inventory sheet.

My blog

http://blog.staffannoteberg.com

I write about the Pomodoro Technique on my blog, but I also write about many other fascinating things.

My Twitter stream

http://twitter.com/staffannoteberg

Afterword

A3.1 Myself

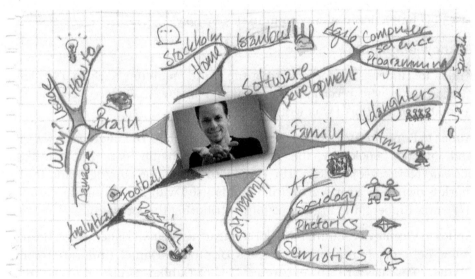

My name is Staffan. I live in Stockholm and Istanbul with my wife Anni and our four daughters, Thea, Edda, Groa, and Bina. Two decades ago, I studied mathematics and computer science at the Royal Institute of Technology in Stockholm. But I started programming many years before that. My first computer was a Commodore 64, a machine that looked like a bread tin.

Some years ago I read Francesco Cirillo's book about the Pomodoro Technique,[1] and I started practicing it. Then I began to teach this methodology, and now I'm writing a book about it.

I'd love to hear your stories and experiences of using the Pomodoro Technique. Don't hesitate to send an email to staffan.noteberg@rekursiv.se or connect with me in social network services like Twitter, LinkedIn or Facebook. You'll find me at AIM, Dopplr, Facebook, Flickr, FriendFeed, Friendster, GTalk, ICQ, LinkedIn, MSN/Live, MySpace, Plaxo, Slideshare, Twitter, Xing, Yahoo, and probably half a dozen more communities by now.

A3.2 Acknowledgments

Kudos to Tindersticks for recording the *Curtains* album back in 1997 and Mercan Dede who recorded the *Su* album in 2003. They've been on the turntable all the time I was writing this book.

Kudos to Francesco Cirillo for inventing the Pomodoro Technique. His website and original book on the Pomodoro Technique can be found at http://www.pomodorotechnique.com. The Pomodoro Technique copyright and trademark is owned by Francesco Cirillo and is used with his permission. Kudos to Henrik Kniberg and Francesco for contributing the forewords.

Kudos to Vicente Ayestarán, Patrick Baumgartner, Simon Baker, Chris Beams, Isidor Behrens, Renzo Borgatti, Hans Brattberg, Daniel Brolund, Tommy Bryntse, Pascal Van Cauwenberghe, Mikael Dahlke, Brian Di Croce, Karl Dickson, Åsa Dickson, Ola Ellnestam, Dan Fernandez, Sebastian Ganslandt, Robert Ginsberg, Tormod Halvorsen, Chris Hedgate, Mats Henricson, Joakim Holm, Peter Hultgren, César Idrovo, Bent Jensen, Joakim Karlsson, Dave Klein, Pekka Klärck, Lasse Koskela, Jeff Kwak, Melanie Langenhan, Andreas Larsson, Eric Lefevre, Ralf Lippold, Brian McKeough, Karl Métivier, Gustaf Nilsson Kotte, Anders Nilsson, Michael Nilsson, Thomas Nilsson, Viktor Nordling, Lena Norman, Bernard Notarianni, Jack Nutting, Joakim Ohlrogge, Jelena Vencl Ohlrogge, Libin Pan, Tomas Rahkonen, Johanna Rothman, Magnus Rydin, Johan Rylander, Måns Sandström, Kevin E. Schlabach, Peter

---

1.   http://www.pomodorotechnique.com

Sönnergren, Antonio Terreno, Thomas Thyberg, Portia Tung, Jacques Turbé, Kevin Walton, Tsutomu Yasui, and Jason Yip for reviewing the draft.

Kudos to Daniel H Steinberg, Steve Peter, Kim Wimpsett, Janet Furlow, and the other people at Pragmatic Bookshelf for transforming the manuscript into a real book.

Infinite kudos to AIK: *alltid är vi med er, alltid ska vi se er.*

A3.3 Colophon

I made the drawings in an A6, top-spiral, 80-sheet pad from Esselte. It is Nordic Swan environmentally labeled and has 5x5 mm squares, no holes, and wood-free 60 gr/m2 paper.

I did the pencil drawings with a BIC Matic mechanical pencil with 0.7 mm HB leads. Then I added watercolor from a Color & Co paint set filled with six tempera blocks in size 2 (diameter 57 mm, height 19 mm) in the following colors: Gold Yellow, Carmine, Ultramarine, Brilliant Green, Black, and White. Finally, I scanned them with a HP Photosmart 1200 Photo Scanner in 300 dpi, 24-bit color.

The spiral pad, the mechanical pencil, the watercolor paint set, and the photo scanner are all inexpensive, simple tools. I'm convinced that the content, the ideas, and the way something is explained is more important than the quality, the sophistication, and the price of the tools.

The body type in this book is Bookman, designed in 1936 by Chauncey Griffith of American Type Founders, based on a design by Alexander Phemister. The current version is a digital revival by Ed Benguiat for the International Typeface Corporation in 1975.

Headings are Avant Garde, designed by Herb Lubalin as the logo for *Avant Garde* magazine and developed into a typeface by Lubalin and Tom Carnase in the early 1970s.

Bibliography

[AK53]   Eugène Aserinsky and Nathaniel Kleitman. Regularly Occurring Periods
           of Eye Motility, and Concomitant Phenomena, during Sleep. *Science*.
           118[3062]:273–274, 1953.

[All02]   David Allen. *Getting Things Done: The Art of Stress-Free Productivity*. Penguin
           Group (USA) Incorporated, USA, 2002.

[BB96]   Tony Buzan and Barry Buzan. *The Mind Map Book: How to Use Radiant
           Thinking to Maximize Your Brain's Untapped Potential*. Plume, New York,
           NY, USA, 1996.

[Bab08]   Leo Babauta. *Zen To Done: The Ultimate Simple Productivity System*. Create
           Space, Scotts Valley, CA, 2008.

[Bad66]   Alan Baddeley. Short-term memory for word sequences as a function of
           acoustic, semantic and formal similarity. *Quarterly Journal of Experimental
           Psychology*. 18, 1966.

[Bec00]   Kent Beck. *Extreme Programming Explained: Embrace Change*. Addison-
           Wesley Longman, Reading, MA, 2000.

[Bra08]   Nicole Branan. Go Ahead, Change Your Mind. *Scientific American Mind*.
           19:5, 2008.

[Buz03]   Tony Buzan. *Brain Child*. Thorsons, London, UK, 2003.

[Cir06]   Francesco Cirillo. *The Pomodoro Technique*. Portfolio Hardcover, USA, 2006.

[Cov94]   Stephen R. Covey. *The 7 Habits of Highly Effective People*. The Free Press,
           New York, NY, 1994.

[Csi02]   Mihaly Csikszentmihalyi. *Flow*. Random House, New York, NY, USA, 2002.

[EHPT07]   Jeffrey M. Ellenbogen, Peter T. Hu, Jessica D. Payne, Debra Titone, and
           Matthew P. Walker. Human relational memory requires time and sleep.

> *Proceedings of the National Academy of Sciences of the United States of America.* 104(18), 2007.

[Fio07]   Neil A. Fiore. *The Now Habit.* Jeremy P Tarcher, New York, USA, Rev Ed, 2007.

[For00]   Mark Forster. *Get Everything Done.* Hodder & Stoughton, London, UK, 2000.

[Fre08]   Sigmund Freud. *5s Kaizen.* Management Books 2000, Cirencester, UK, 2008.

[Fre80]   Sigmund Freud. *The Interpretation of Dreams.* Avon Books, Dresden, Tennessee, 1980.

[Gla06]   Malcolm Gladwell. *Blink.* Little, Brown and Company, New York, NY, USA, 2006.

[Gla08]   Malcolm Gladwell. *Outliers: The Story of Success.* Little, Brown and Company, New York, NY, USA, 2008.

[Gol04]   Eliyahu Goldratt. *The Goal.* North River Press, Great Barrington, MA, Third, 2004.

[Ing01]   David H. Ingvar. *Hjärnans futurum.* Atlantis, Stockholm, Sweden, 2001.

[Jö05]   Bodil Jönsson. *Ten Thoughts About Time.* Robinson Publishing, London, UK, New, 2005.

[Kli08]   Torkel Klingberg. *The Overflowing Brain.* Oxford University Press, New York, NY, 2008.

[Lin08]   Joakim Lindström. *Hjärnkoll.* Bonnier Carlsen, Stockholm, Sweden, 2008.

[Mor98]   Hans Moravec. When will computer hardware match the human brain?. *Journal of Transhumanism.* 1, 1998.

[Rev09]   William Reville. *What autism tells us about development of savant skills.* www.theautismnews.com, www.theautismnews.com, 2009.

[Rot09]   Johanna Rothman. *Manage Your Project Portfolio: Increase Your Capacity and Finish More Projects.* The Pragmatic Bookshelf, Raleigh, NC and Dallas, TX, 2009.

[Sch04]   Ken Schwaber. *Agile Project Management with Scrum.* Microsoft Press, Redmond, WA, 2004.

[Sch05]   Barry Schwartz. *The Paradox of Choice: Why More Is Less.* Harper Perennial Modern Classics, New York, NY, USA, 2005.

[Sen94]   Peter M. Senge. *The Fifth Discipline: The Art & Practice of the Learning Organization* . Doubleday, New York, NY, USA, 1994.

[Sur05]   James Surowiecki. *The Wisdom of Crowds*. Anchor, New York, NY, USA, 2005.

[Tam06]   Daniel Tammet. *Born on a Blue Day: A Memoir of Aspergers and an Extraordinary Mind*. Hodder & Stoughton, London, UK, 2006.

Redesign Your Career

Ready to kick your career up to the next level? Time to rewire your brain and then reinvigorate your job itself.

Software development happens in your head. Not in an editor, IDE, or design tool. You're well educated on how to work with software and hardware, but what about *wetware*—our own brains? Learning new skills and new technology is critical to your career, and it's all in your head.

In this book by Andy Hunt, you'll learn how our brains are wired, and how to take advantage of your brain's architecture. You'll learn new tricks and tips to learn more, faster, and retain more of what you learn.

You need a pragmatic approach to thinking and learning. You need to *Refactor Your Wetware*.

Andy Hunt
(290 pages) ISBN: 9781934356050. $34.95
http://pragprog.com/book/ahptl

This book is about creating a remarkable career in software development. In most cases, remarkable careers don't come by chance. They require thought, intention, action, and a willingness to change course when you've made mistakes. Most of us have been stumbling around letting our careers take us where they may. It's time to take control. This revised and updated second edition lays out a strategy for planning and creating a radically successful life in software development.

Chad Fowler
(232 pages) ISBN: 9781934356340. $23.95
http://pragprog.com/book/cfcar2

The Joy of Math and Healthy Programming

Rediscover the joy and fascinating weirdness of pure mathematics, and learn how to take a healthier approach to programming.

Mathematics is beautiful—and it can be fun and exciting as well as practical. *Good Math* is your guide to some of the most intriguing topics from two thousand years of mathematics: from Egyptian fractions to Turing machines; from the real meaning of numbers to proof trees, group symmetry, and mechanical computation. If you've ever wondered what lay beyond the proofs you struggled to complete in high school geometry, or what limits the capabilities of the computer on your desk, this is the book for you.

Mark C. Chu-Carroll
(282 pages) ISBN: 9781937785338. $34
http://pragprog.com/book/mcmath

To keep doing what you love, you need to maintain your own systems, not just the ones you write code for. Regular exercise and proper nutrition help you learn, remember, concentrate, and be creative—skills critical to doing your job well. Learn how to change your work habits, master exercises that make working at a computer more comfortable, and develop a plan to keep fit, healthy, and sharp for years to come.

This book is intended only as an informative guide for those wishing to know more about health issues. In no way is this book intended to replace, countermand, or conflict with the advice given to you by your own healthcare provider including Physician, Nurse Practitioner, Physician Assistant, Registered Dietician, and other licensed professionals.

Joe Kutner
(254 pages) ISBN: 9781937785314. $36
http://pragprog.com/book/jkthp

Be Agile

Don't just "do" agile; you want to *be* agile. We'll show you how.

The best agile book isn't a book: *Agile in a Flash* is a unique deck of index cards that fit neatly in your pocket. You can tape them to the wall. Spread them out on your project table. Get stains on them over lunch. These cards are meant to be used, not just read.

Jeff Langr and Tim Ottinger
(110 pages) ISBN: 9781934356715. $15
http://pragprog.com/book/olag

Here are three simple truths about software development:

1. You can't gather all the requirements up front. 2. The requirements you do gather will change. 3. There is always more to do than time and money will allow.

Those are the facts of life. But you can deal with those facts (and more) by becoming a fierce software-delivery professional, capable of dispatching the most dire of software projects and the toughest delivery schedules with ease and grace.

Jonathan Rasmusson
(280 pages) ISBN: 9781934356586. $34.95
http://pragprog.com/book/jtrap

The Pragmatic Bookshelf

The Pragmatic Bookshelf features books written by developers for developers. The titles continue the well-known Pragmatic Programmer style and continue to garner awards and rave reviews. As development gets more and more difficult, the Pragmatic Programmers will be there with more titles and products to help you stay on top of your game.

Visit Us Online

This Book's Home Page
http://pragprog.com/book/snfocus
Source code from this book, errata, and other resources. Come give us feedback, too!

Register for Updates
http://pragprog.com/updates
Be notified when updates and new books become available.

Join the Community
http://pragprog.com/community
Read our weblogs, join our online discussions, participate in our mailing list, interact with our wiki, and benefit from the experience of other Pragmatic Programmers.

New and Noteworthy
http://pragprog.com/news
Check out the latest pragmatic developments, new titles and other offerings.

Save on the eBook

Save on the eBook versions of this title. Owning the paper version of this book entitles you to purchase the electronic versions at a terrific discount.

PDFs are great for carrying around on your laptop—they are hyperlinked, have color, and are fully searchable. Most titles are also available for the iPhone and iPod touch, Amazon Kindle, and other popular e-book readers.

Buy now at *http://pragprog.com/coupon*

Contact Us

Online Orders:	*http://pragprog.com/catalog*
Customer Service:	*support@pragprog.com*
International Rights:	*translations@pragprog.com*
Academic Use:	*academic@pragprog.com*
Write for Us:	*http://pragprog.com/write-for-us*
Or Call:	+1 800-699-7764